Tin Whistle

FOR BEGINNERS

Volume 1

Irish Songs
Gaelic Songs
Scottish Songs

To download the audio to accompany this book, please see the site : http://wb1.tradschool.com

Arrangements by Stephen Ducke
Web www.tradschool.com
Email info@tradschool.com

Copyright © 2016 Stephen Ducke. All rights reserved

Contents

Part 1 : Irish Folk Songs..................5
   The Good Ship Kangaroo..................6
   Botany Bay..................7
   Arthur McBride..................8
   The Harp that Once..................10
   The Boys of Fairhill..................11
   Follow Me Up to Carlow..................12
   The Wild Rover..................14
   Boolavogue..................16
   The Rare Old Mountain Dew..................18
   The Well Below the Valley..................20
   The Cliffs of Dooneen..................22
   Do You Love an Apple..................23
   The Waxie's Dargle..................24
   High Germany..................25
   The Galway Races..................26
   Johnny I Hardly Know Ye..................28
   Danny Boy..................30
   I'll Tell My Ma..................32
   The Bantry Girl's Lament..................33
   Galway Bay..................34
   Lanigan's Ball..................36
   The Last Rose of Summer..................38
   The Rising of the Moon..................39
   The Lark in the Morning..................40
   A Bunch of Thyme..................42
   The Leaving of Liverpool..................43
   The Black Velvet Band..................44
   Whiskey in the Jar..................46
   Down by the Glenside..................48
   Weile Waile..................50

Part 2 - Irish Gaelic Songs..................51
   An bhfaca tú mo Shéamaisín?..................52
   An cailín rua..................53
   An seanduine dóite..................54
   Báidín fheilimí..................55
   Bean Pháidín..................56
   Cuaichín Ghleann Néifin..................57
   Cill Cháis..................58
   Éamonn an chnoic..................60
   Cúnla..................62
   Jimmy mo mhíle stór..................63
   Eibhlín a rún..................64
   Óró! 'sé do bheatha 'bhaile..................65
   Níl 'na lá..................66
   Nead na lachan sa mhúta..................67
   Siúil a rún..................68
   Siúbhán Ní Dhuibhir..................69

   An spailpín fánach..................70
   Thugamar féin an samhradh linn..................71
   Déirín dé..................72
   Cailleach an airgid..................73
   An maidrín rua..................74
   Trasna na dtonnta..................75
   Óró mo bháidín..................76
   Cailin na gruaige doinne..................78
   Ar éirinn ní n-eósainn cé h-í..................80
   Beidh aonach amárach..................82
   Tá mé i mo shuí..................84
   Buachaill ón Éirne..................85
   Dúlamán na binne buí..................86
   Bheir mé ó..................87

Part 3 - Scottish Folk Songs..................89
   Gin I Were..................90
   Wild Mountain Thyme..................91
   Scots Wha Hae..................92
   Ye Banks and Braes..................93
   My Bonnie Lies Over the Ocean..................94
   Coming Through the Rye..................96
   Green Grow the Rashes O..................97
   Katie Bairdie..................98
   Loch Lomond..................99
   The Campbells are Coming..................100
   The Calton Weaver..................101
   Come O'er the Stream, Charlie..................102
   Aiken Drum..................104
   The Gypsy Laddies..................105
   Charlie is My Darling..................106
   The Four Marys..................26
   The Blue Bells of Scotland..................108
   All the Blue Bonnets..................109
   The Bonnie Banks of the Roses..................110
   The Skye Boat Song..................111
   Wae's Me for Prince Charlie..................112
   Dance to your Daddy..................113
   McPherson's Rant..................114
   The Barnyards of Delgaty..................115
   The Cradle Song..................116
   Scotland the Brave..................117
   The Bonnie Lass o'Fyvie..................118
   Will Ye No Come Back Again?..................120
   The Braes o'Killiecrankie..................121
   John Peel..................122

Appendix : Playing the Tin Whistle..................123
Index..................126

PART 1 : IRISH FOLK SONGS

The Good Ship Kangaroo

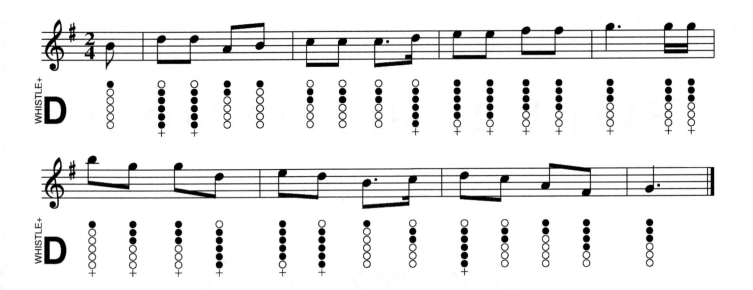

Once I was a waiting man who lived at home at ease
Now I am a mariner that ploughs the stormy seas
I always loved seafaring life I bid my love adieu
I shipped as steward and cook me boys on board the kangaroo

I never thought she would prove false or either prove untrue
As we sailed away from Milford Bay on board the Kangaroo

Think of me oh think of me she mournfully did say
When you are in a foreign land and I am far away
And take this lucky thrupenny bit it will make you bear in mind
This loving trusting faithful heart you left in tears behind

Cheer up, cheer up my own true love don't weep so bitterly
She sobbed she sighed she choked she cried till she could not say goodbye
I won't be gone for very long but for a month or two
And when I return again of course I'll visit you

Our ship it was homeward bound from many's the foreign shore
Many's the foreign present unto my love I bore
I brought tortoises from Tenerife and ties from Timbuktu
A China rat, a Bengal cat and a Bombay cockatoo

Paid off I sought her dwelling on a street above the town
Where an ancient dame upon the line was hanging out her gown
Where is my love? she's vanished sir about six months ago
With a smart young man who drives the van for Chaplin Son & Co.

Here's a health to dreams of married life to soap suds and blue
Heart's true love, patent starch and washing soda too
Ill go into some foreign shore no longer can I stay
With some China Hottentot I'll throw my life away

My love she was no foolish girl her age it was two score
My love she was no spinster she'd been married twice before
I cannot say it was her wealth that stole my heart away
She was a washer in the laundry for one and nine a day

Botany Bay

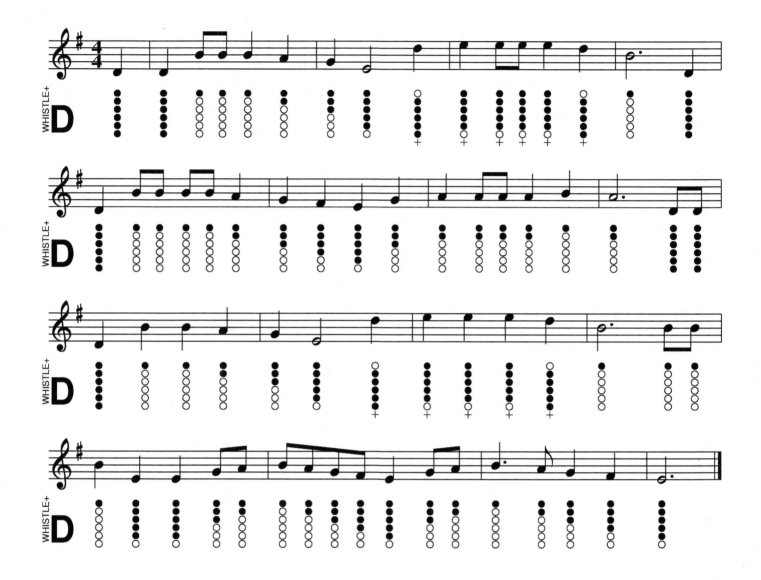

Farewell to your bricks and mortar, farewell to your dirty lies
Farewell to your gangers and gang planks
And to hell with your overtime
For the good ship Ragamuffin, she's lying at the quay
For to take oul' Pat with a shovel on his back
To the shores of Botany Bay

I'm on my way down to the quay, where the ship at anchor lays
To command a gang of navvies, that they told me to engage
I thought I'd drop in for a drink before I went away
For to take a trip on an emigrant ship to the shores of Botany Bay,
To the shores of botany bay

The boss came up this morning, he says "Well, Pat you know
If you don't get your navvies out, I'm afraid you'll have to go"
So I asked him for my wages and demanded all my pay
For I told him straight, I'm going to emigrate to the shores of Botany Bay

And when I reach Australia I'll go and look for gold
There's plenty there for the digging of, or so I have been told
Or else I'll go back to my trade and a hundred bricks I'll lay
Because I live for an eight hour shift on the shores of Botany Bay

www.tradschool.com

Arthur McBride

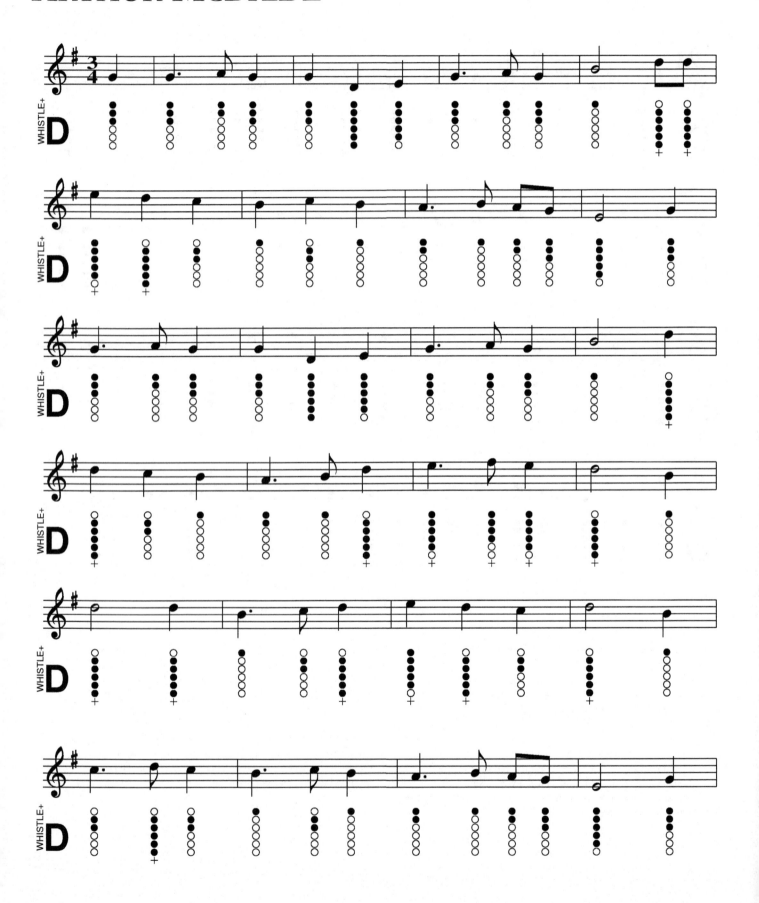

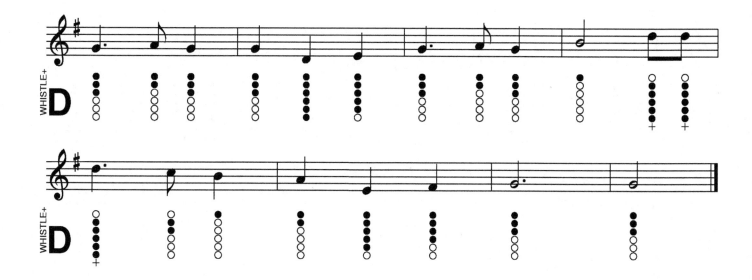

I had a first cousin called Arthur McBride
He and I took a stroll down by the by the sea side
A seeking good fortune and what might be tide
'Twas just as the day was a dawning
After resting we both took a tramp
We met Sergeant Harper and Corporal Cramp
Besides the wee drummer who beat up for camp
With his rowdy dow dow in the morning

Says he me young fellows if you will enlist
A guinea you quickly have in your fist
Likewise the crown for to kick the dust
And drink the king's health in the morning
From a soldier he leads a very fine life
He always is blessed with a charming young wife
And he pays all his debts without sorrow or strife
And always lives happy and charming

Ah now me bold sergeant we are not for sale
We'll make no such bargain, your bribe won't avail
We're not tried of our country we don't care to sail
Although that your offer is charming
And if we were such fools as to take the advance
This right bloody slander would be our poor chance
For the Queen wouldn't scruple to send us to France
Where we would be shot with out warning

He says me young fellows if I hear but one word
I instantly now will out with my sword
And into your body as strength will afford
So now my gay devils take warning
But Arthur and I we took in the odds
We gave them no chance for to launch out their swords
Our whacking shillelaghs came over their heads
And paid them right smart in the morning

As for the wee drummer we rifled his pouch
And we made a foot- ball of his rowdy dow dow
And into the ocean to rock and to roll
And bade it a tedious returning
As for the old rapier that hung by his side
We flung it as far as we could in tide
To devil I pitch you said Arthur McBride
To temper your steel in the morning

www.tradschool.com

The Harp that Once

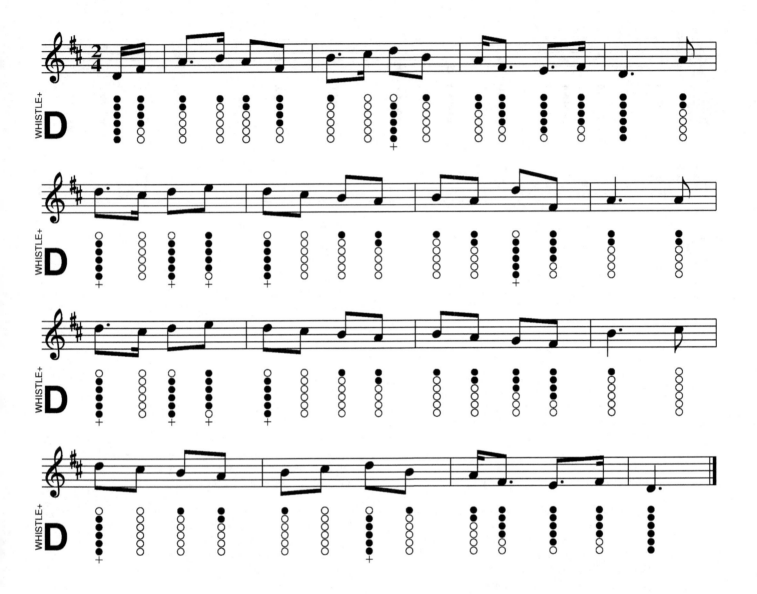

The harp that once through Tara's halls
The soul of music shed,
Now hangs as mute on Tara's walls,
As if that soul were fled. --
So sleeps the pride of former days,
So glory's thrill is o'er,
And hearts, that once beat high for praise,
Now feel that pulse no more.

No more to chiefs and ladies bright
The harp of Tara swells;
The chord alone, that breaks at night,
Its tale of ruin tells.
Thus Freedom now so seldom wakes,
The only throb she gives,
Is when some heart indignant breaks,
To show that still she lives.

The Boys of Fairhill

The smell on Patrick's Bridge is wicked
How does Father Matthew stick it?
Here's up them all says the boys of Fairhill

The Blarney hens don't lay at all
And when they lay they lay 'em small
Here's up them all says the boys of Fairhill

The Blackpool girls are very rude
They go swimming in the nude
Here's up them all says the boys of Fairhill

Blackpool boys are very nice
I have tried them once or twice
Here's up them all says the boys of Fairhill

If you come to Cork you'll get drisheen
Murphy's stout and pigs crubeens
Here's up them all says the boys of Fairhill

Well, Christy Ring he hooked the ball
We hooked him up, balls and all
Here's up them all says the boys of Fairhill

Follow Me Up to Carlow

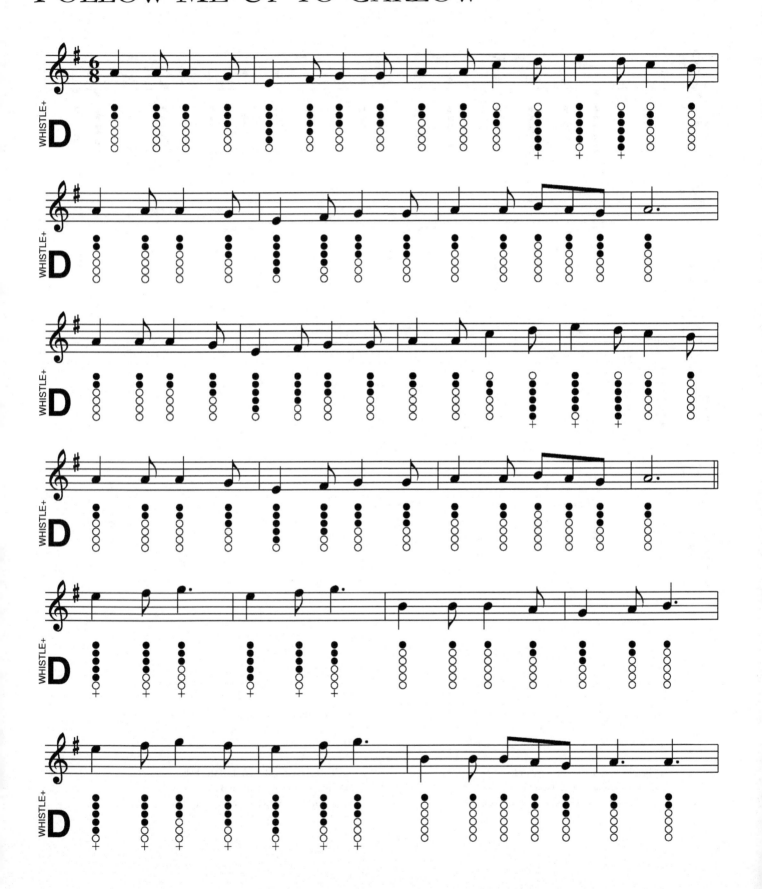

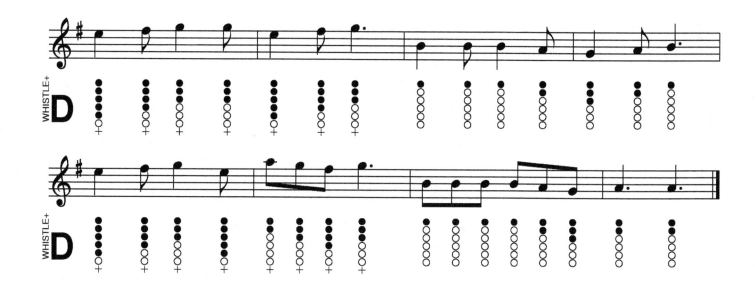

Lift Mac Cahir Og your face,
You're brooding o'er the old disgrace
That Black Fitzwilliam stormed your place
and drove you to the ferns
Gray said victory was sure,
And soon the firebrand he'd secure
Until he met at Glenmalure
with Fiach McHugh O'Byrne

Curse and swear, Lord Kildare,
Fiach will do what Fiach will dare
Now Fitzwilliam have a care,
Fallen is your star low
Up with halberd, out with sword,
on we go for, by the Lord
Fiach McHugh has given the word
"Follow me up to Carlow"

See the swords of Glen Imaal,
They're flashing o'er the English Pale
See all the childer of the Gael,
Beneath O'Byrne's banner
Rooster of the fighting stock,
Would you let a Saxon cock
Crow out upon an Irish Rock,
Fly up and teach him manners

From Tassagart to Clonmore,
There flows a stream of Saxon gore
And great is Rory Og O'More
At sending loons to Hades
White is sick and Gray is fled,
And now for black Fitzwilliam's head
We'll send it over, dripping red
to Liza and her ladies

The Wild Rover

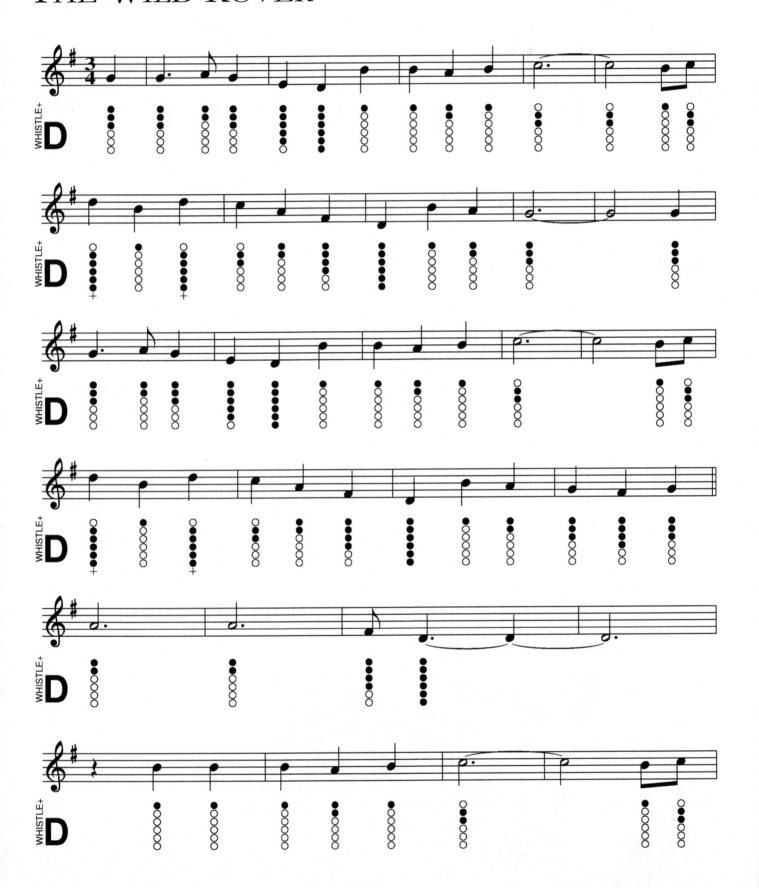

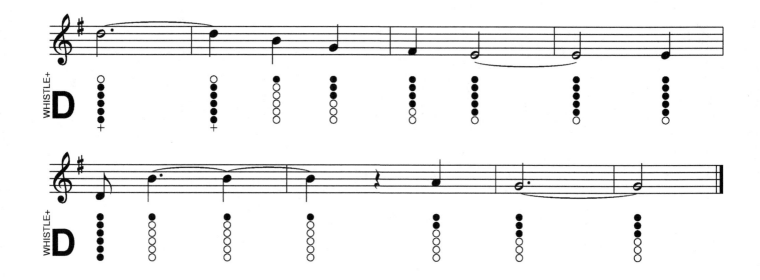

I've been a wild rover for many's the year
I've spent all me money on whiskey and beer
But now I'm returning with gold in great store
And I never will play the wild rover no more

And it's no, nay, never,
No, nay never no more
Will I play the wild rover,
No never no more

I went in to an alehouse I used to frequent
And I told the landlady me money was spent
I asked her for credit, she answered me nay
Such a customer as you I can have any day

I took up from my pocket, ten sovereigns bright
And the landlady's eyes opened wide with delight
She says "I have whiskeys and wines of the best
And the words that you told me were only in jest"

I'll go home to my parents, confess what I've done
And I'll ask them to pardon their prodigal son
And, when they've caressed me as oft times before
I never will play the wild rover no more

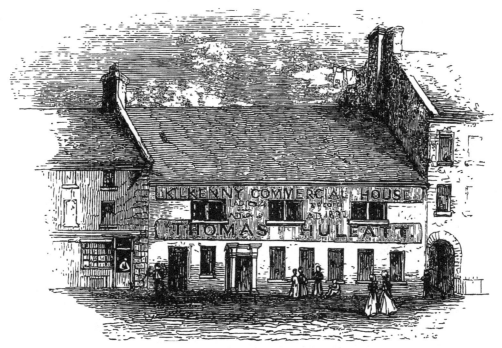

Boolavogue

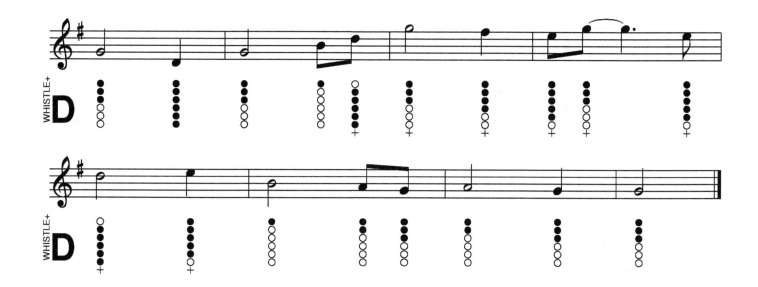

At Boolavogue as the sun was setting,
O'er the bright may meadows of Shelmalier,
A rebel hand set the heather blazing,
and brought the neighbours from far and near;

Then Father Murphy from old Kilcormack
Spurred up the rock with a warning cry:
"Arm! Arm!" he cried, "For I've come to lead you,
for Ireland`s freedom we'll fight or die!"

He lead us on against the coming soldiers,
And the cowardly Yeomen we put to flight,
'Twas at the Harrow the boys of Wexford
Showed Bookey`s regiment how men could fight;

Look out for hirelings, King George of England,
Search every kingdom where breathes a slave,
For Father Murphy of County Wexford,
Sweeps o'er the land like a mighty wave.

We took Camolin and Enniscorthy,
And Wexford storming drove out our foes,
'Twas at Slieve Coilte our pikes were reeking
With the crimson blood of the beaten Yeos.

At Tubberneering and Ballyellis,
Full many a Hessian lay in his gore,
Ah! Father Murphy had aid come over,
The Green Flag floated from shore to shore!

At Vinegar Hill o`er the pleasant Slaney,
Our heroes vainly stood back to back,
and the Yeos at Tullow took Father Murphy,
and burnt his body upon a rack.

God grant you glory, brave Father Murphy,
And open Heaven to all your men,
the cause that called you may call tomorrow,
in another fight for the Green again.

The Rare Old Mountain Dew

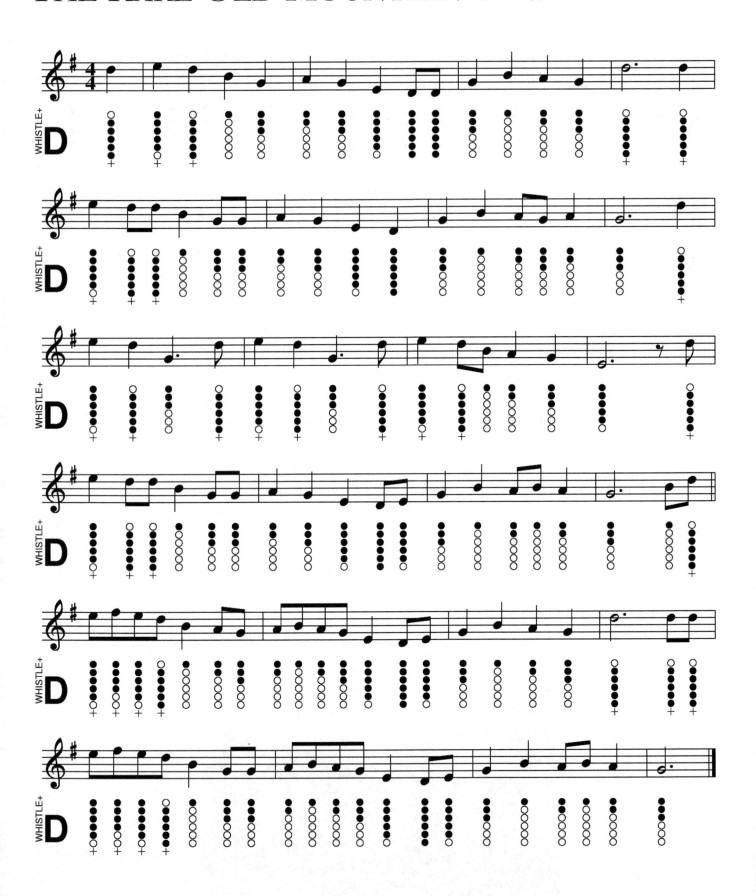

Let grasses and waters flow in a free and easy way,
But give me enough of the rare old stuff that's brewed near Galway Bay,
Come policemen all from Donegal, Sligo and Leitrim too,
Oh, we'll give them the slip and we'll take a sip
Of the rare old Mountain Dew

Hi di-diddly-idle-um, diddly-doodle-idle-um, diddly-doo-ri-diddlum-deh
Hi di-diddly-idle-um, diddly-doodle-idle-um, diddly-doo-ri-diddlum-deh

At the foot of the hill there's a neat little still,
Where the smoke curls up to the sky,
By the smoke and the smell you can plainly tell
That there's poitin brewing nearby.
For it fills the air with a perfume rare,
And betwixt both me and you,
As home we troll, we can take a bowl,
Or a bucket of the Mountain Dew

Now learned men who use the pen,
Have sung the praises high
Of the rare poitin from Ireland green,
Distilled from wheat and rye.
Put away with your pills, it'll cure all ills,
Be ye Pagan, Christian or Jew,
So take off your coat and grease your throat
With a bucket of the Mountain Dew.

The Well Below the Valley

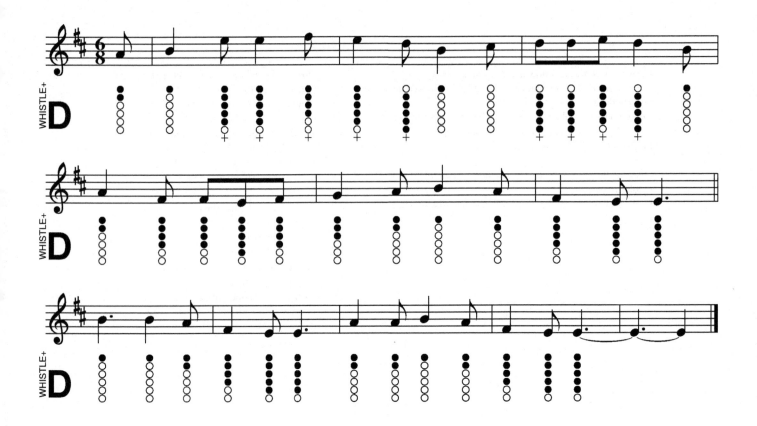

Green grows the lily-o
Right among the bushes-o

A gentleman was passing by
And he asked for a drink as he was dry
At the well below the valley-o
Green grows the lily-o
Right among the bushes-o

My cup is full up to the brim
And if I were to stoop I might fall in
At the well below the valley-o
Green grows the lily-o
Right among the bushes-o

If your true love was passing by
You'd fill him a drink if he was dry
At the well below the valley-o
Green grows the lily-o
Right among the bushes-o

She swore by grass, she swore by corn
Her true love had never been born
At the well below the valley-o
Green grows the lily-o
Right among the bushes-o

He said to her you're swearing wrong
Six fine children you've had born
At the well below the valley-o
Green grows the lily-o
Right among the bushes-o

If you be a man of noble fame
You'll tell to me the father of them
At the well below the valley-o
Green grows the lily-o
Right among the bushes-o

There's one of them by your brother John
At the well below the valley-o
One of them by your Uncle Don
At the well below the valley-o
Two of them by your father dear
At the well below the valley-o
Green grows the lily-o
Right among the bushes-o

If you be a man of noble fame
You'll tell to me what did happen to them
At the well below the valley-o
Green grows the lily-o
Right among the bushes-o

There's one of them buried beneath the tree
At the well below the valley-o
Another two buried beneath the stone
At the well below the valley-o
Two of them outside the graveyard wall
At the well below the valley-o
Green grows the lily-o
Right among the bushes-o

If you be a man of noble fame
You'll tell to me what will happen myself
At the well below the valley-o
Green grows the lily-o
Right among the bushes-o

You'll be seven years a-ringing a bell
At the well below the valley-o
And seven years a-burning in hell
At the well below the valley-o

I'll be seven years a-ringing a bell
But the Lord above may save my soul
From burning in hell at the well below the valley-o
Green grows the lily-o
Right among the bushes-o
Green grows the lily-o
Right among the bushes-o

The Cliffs of Dooneen

You may travel far far from your own native home
Far away across the mountains far away o'er the foam
But of all the fine places that I've ever seen,
There's none to compare with The Cliffs of Dooneen

Take a view o'er the water fine sights you'll see there
You'll see the high rocky slopes on the West coast of Clare
The towns of Kilrush and Kilkee can be seen
From the high rocky slopes at The Cliffs of Dooneen

Its a nice place to be on a fine Summer's day
Watching all the wild flowers that ne'er do decay
The hare and lofty pheasant are plain to be seen
Making homes for their young round The Cliffs of Dooneen

Fare thee well to Dooneen fare thee well for a while
And to all the fine people I'm leaving behind
To the streams and the meadows where late I have been
And the high rocky slopes of The Cliffs of Dooneen

Do You Love an Apple

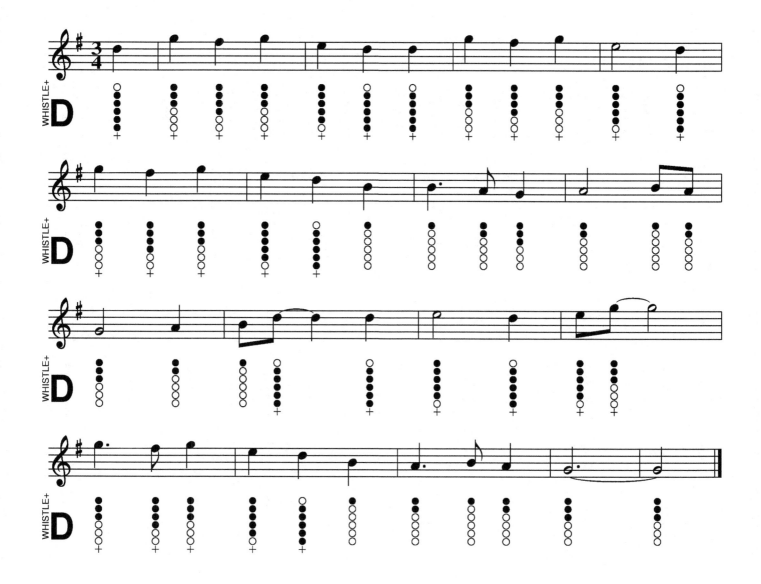

Do you love an apple, do you love a pear?
Do you love a laddie with curly brown hair?
And still, I love him, I can't deny him
I'll be with him where ever he goes

Before I got married I wore a black shawl
But now that I'm married I wear bugger-all
And still I love him…

He stood at the corner, a fag in his mouth
Two hands in his pockets, he whistled me out
And still I love him…

He works at the pier, for nine pound a week,
Saturday night he comes rolling home drunk
And still I love him…

Before I got married I'd sport and I'd play
But now, the cradle gets in me way
And still I love him…

Do you love an apple, do you love a pear?
Do you love a laddie with curly brown hair?
And still, I love him, I can't deny him
I'll be with him where ever he goes

The Waxie's Dargle

Says my auld one to your auld one
Will you come to the Waxie's dargle
Says your auld one to my auld one
Sure I haven't got a farthing
I've just been down to Monto town
To see Uncle McArdle
But he wouldn't lend me a half a crown
To go to the Waxie's dargle

What'll you have, will you have a pint
Yes, I'll have a pint with you, sir
And if one of us doesn't order soon
We'll be thrown out of the boozer

Says my auld one to your auld one
Will you come to the Galway races
Says your auld one to my auld one
With the price of my auld lad's braces
I went down to Capel Street
To the pawn shop money lenders
But they wouldn't give me a couple of bob
On my auld lad's red suspenders

Says my auld one to your auld one
We've got no beef nor mutton
But if we go down to Monto town
We might get a drink for nothing
Here's a piece of good advice
I got from an auld fish-monger
When food is scarce and you see the hearse
You'll know you've died of hunger

High Germany

Oh Willy love, oh Willy come list to what I say
My feet they are so tender, I can not march away
And besides my dearest Willy I am with child by thee
Not fitted for the war me love in High Germany

I'll buy for you a horse me love and on it you shall ride
And all my life I'll be there riding by your side
We'll stop at every ale-house and drink when we are dry
We'll be true to one another, get married bye and bye

Oh cursed be the cruel wars that ever they should rise
And out of merry England press many a man likewise
They pressed my true love from me, likewise my brothers three
And sent them to the wars me lad in High Germany

My friends I do not value nor my foes I do not fear
Now my love has left me I wander far and near
And when my baby it is born and smiling on my knee
I'll think of lovely Willy in High Germany

The Galway Races

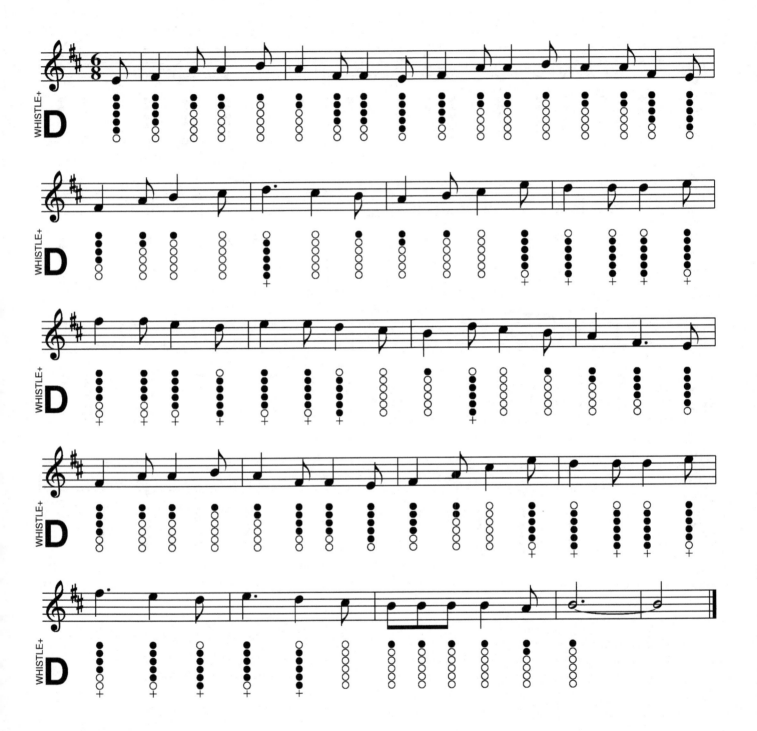

As I went down to Galway Town
To seek for recreation
On the seventeenth of August
Me mind being elevated
There were passengers assembled
With their tickets at the station
And me eyes began to dazzle
And they off to see the races

With me wack fol the do fol
The diddle idle day

There were passengers from Limerick
And passengers from Nenagh
The boys of Connemara
And the Clare unmarried maiden
There were people from Cork City
Who were loyal, true and faithful
Who brought home the Fenian prisoners
From dying in foreign nations

And it's there you'll see the pipers
And the fiddlers competing
And the sporting wheel of fortune
And the four and twenty quarters
And there's others without scruple
Pelting wattles at poor Maggie
And her father well contented
And he gazing at his daughter

And it's there you'll see the jockeys
And they mounted on so stably
The pink, the blue, the orange, and green
The colours of our nation
The time it came for starting
All the horses seemed impatient
Their feet they hardly touched the ground
The speed was so amazing!

There was half a million people there
Of all denominations
The Catholic, the Protestant, the Jew, the Presbyterian
Yet there was no animosity
No matter what persuasion
But failte hospitality
Inducing fresh acquaintance

Johnny I Hardly Know Ye

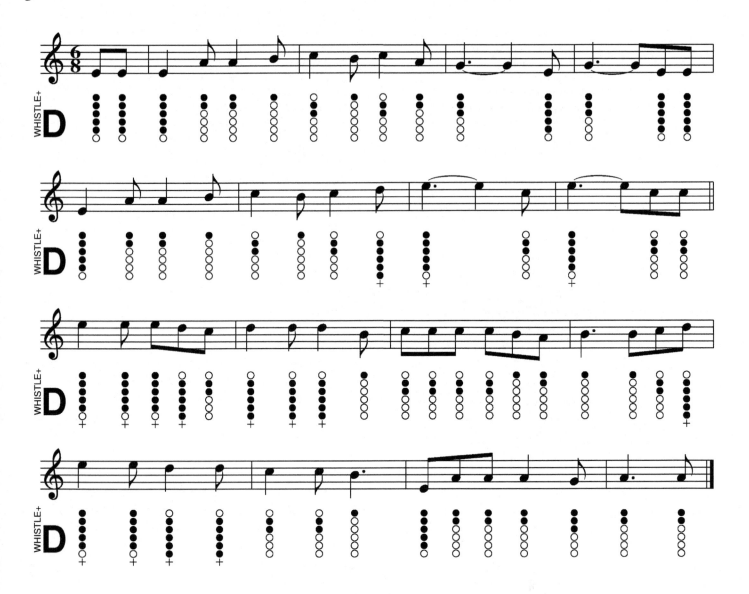

While going the road to sweet Athy, hurroo, hurroo
While going the road to sweet Athy, hurroo, hurroo
While going the road to sweet Athy
A stick in me hand and a tear in me eye
A doleful damsel I heard cry,
Johnny I hardly knew ye.

With your drums and guns and guns and drums, hurroo, hurroo
With your drums and guns and guns and drums, hurroo, hurroo
With your drums and guns and guns and drums
The enemy nearly slew ye
Oh my darling dear, Ye look so queer
Johnny I hardly knew ye.

Where are the eyes that looked so mild, hurroo, hurroo
Where are the eyes that looked so mild, hurroo, hurroo
Where are the eyes that looked so mild
When my poor heart you first beguiled
Why did ye scadaddle from me and the child
Oh Johnny, I hardly knew ye.

Where are your legs that used to run, hurroo, hurroo
Where are your legs that used to run, hurroo, hurroo
Where are your legs that used to run
When you went to carry a gun
Indeed your dancing days are done
Oh Johnny, I hardly knew ye.

I'm happy for to see ye home, hurroo, hurroo
I'm happy for to see ye home, hurroo, hurroo
I'm happy for to see ye home
All from the island of Ceylon
So low in the flesh, so high in the bone
Oh Johnny I hardly knew ye.

Ye haven't an arm, ye haven't a leg, hurroo, hurroo
Ye haven't an arm, ye haven't a leg, hurroo, hurroo
Ye haven't an arm, ye haven't a leg
Ye're an armless, boneless, chickenless egg
Ye'll have to be put with a bowl out to beg
Oh Johnny I hardly knew ye.

They're rolling out the guns again, hurroo, hurroo
They're rolling out the guns again, hurroo, hurroo
They're rolling out the guns again
But they never will take my sons again
No they'll never take my sons again
Johnny I'm swearing to ye.

Danny Boy

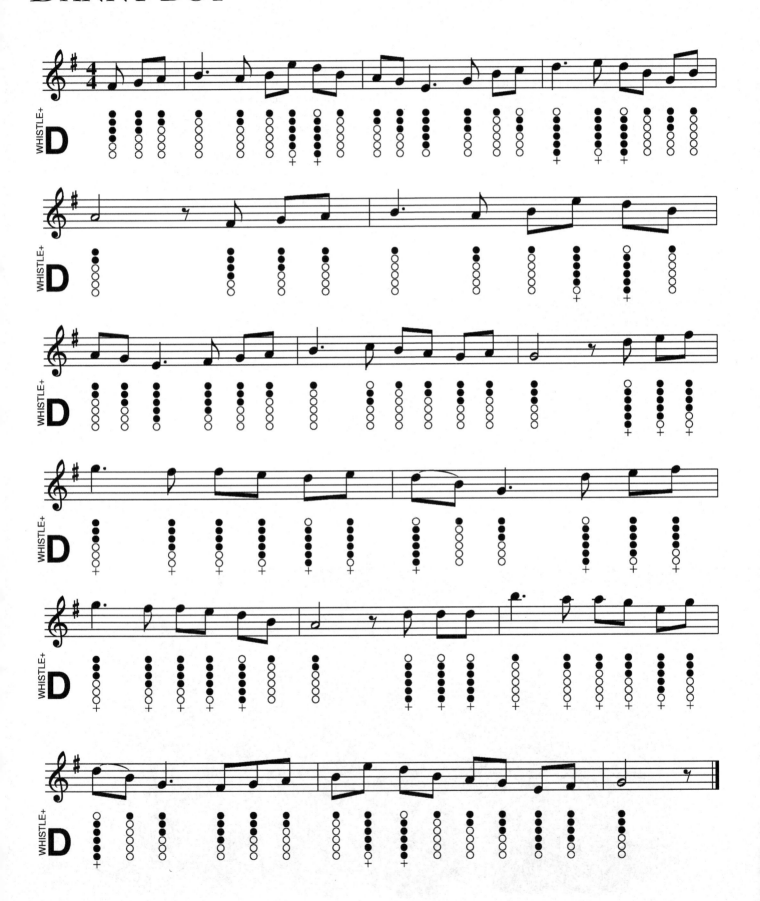

Oh Danny boy, the pipes, the pipes are calling
From glen to glen, and down the mountain side
The summer's gone, and all the flowers are dying
'Tis you, 'tis you must go and I must bide.

But come ye back when summer's in the meadow
Or when the valley's hushed and white with snow
'Tis I'll be here in sunshine or in shadow
Oh Danny boy, oh Danny boy, I love you so.

But when he come, and all the flowers are dying
If I am dead, as dead I well may be
You'll come and find the place where I am lying
And kneel and say an "Ave" there for me.

And I shall hear, tho' soft you tread above me
And all my grave will warm and sweeter be
For you will bend and tell me that you love me
And I shall sleep in peace until you come to

I'll Tell My Ma

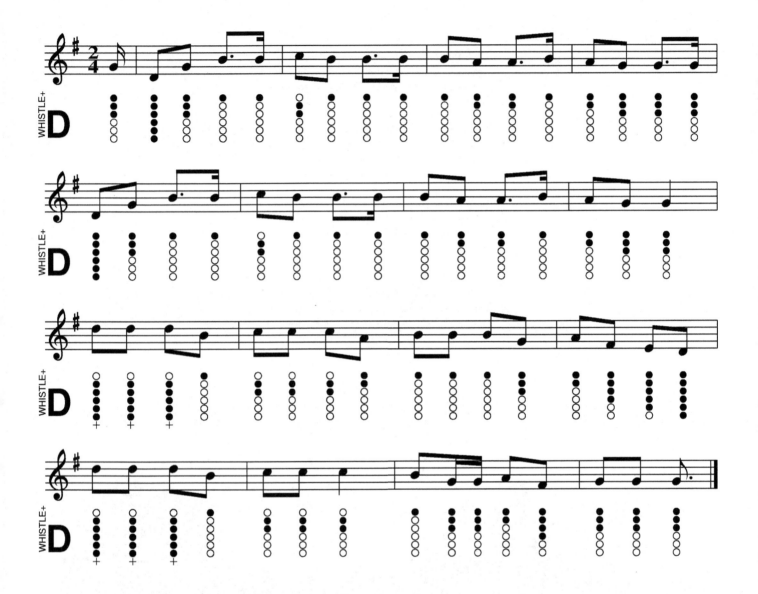

I'll tell me Ma when I go home
The boys won't leave the girls alone.
They pull my hair, they stole my comb,
but that's alright till I go home.

She is handsome, she is pretty
She is the belle of Belfast city
She is courting one, two, three.
Please won't you tell me, who is she?

Albert Mooney says he loves her,
All the boys are fighting for her.
They knock at the door and ring at the bell
Saying "Oh, my true love are you well?"

Out she comes as white as snow,
Rings on her fingers and bells on her toes.
Oul Jenny Murray says she'll die,
If she don't get the fellow with the roving eye.

Let the wind and the rain and the hail blow high
and the snow come tumbling from the sky
She's as nice as apple pie
And she'll get her own lad by and by.
When she gets a lad of her own,
she won't tell her Ma when she goes home
Let them all come as they will
For it's Albert Mooney she loves still.

The Bantry Girl's Lament

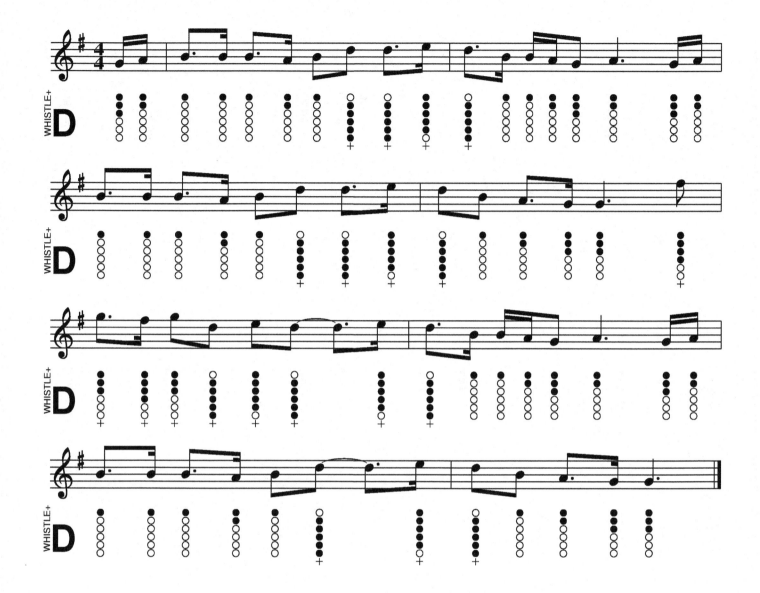

Oh, Who will plough the fields now and who will sow the corn?
Who will mind the sheep now and keep them neatly shorn?
The stack that's in the haggard, unthrashed it may remain
Since Johnny's went a-thrashing the dirty king of Spain

The girls from the bawnogue in sorrow may retire
And the piper and his bellows go home and blow the fire
Since Johnny, lovely Johnny is sailing o'er the main
Along with other patriots to fight the King of Spain

The boys will surely miss him when Moneymore comes round
And they'll find that their bold captain is nowhere to be found
And the peelers must stand idle, all against their will and main
Since the gallant boys who gave them work now peels the King of Spain

At wakes or hurling matches your like we'll never see
Till you come back to us again, *a stór grá geal mo chroí*
And won't you thrash the buckeens that show us much disdain
Because our eyes are not so bright as those you'll meet in Spain

If cruel fate will not permit our Johnny to return
His heavy loss we Bantry girls will never cease to mourn
We'll resign ourselves to our sad lot and die in grief and pain
Since Johnny died for Ireland's pride in the foreign land of Spain

Galway Bay

'Tis far away I am today from scenes I roamed a boy,
And long ago the hour I know I first saw Illinois;
But time nor tide nor waters wide can wean my heart away,
For ever true it flies to you, my dear old Galway Bay.

My chosen bride is by my side, her brown hair silver-grey,
Her daughter Rose as like her grows as April dawn to day.
Our only boy, his mother's joy, his father's pride and stay;
With gifts like these I'd live at ease, were I near Galway Bay.

Oh, grey and bleak, by shore and creek, the rugged rocks abound,
But sweet and green the grass between, as grows on Irish ground,
So friendship fond, all wealth beyond, and love that lives alway,
Bless each poor home beside your foam, my dear old Galway Bay.

A prouder man I'd walk the land in health and peace of mind,
If I might toil and strive and moil, nor cast one thought behind,
But what would be the world to me, its wealth and rich array,
If memory I lost of thee, my own dear Galway Bay.

Had I youth's blood and hopeful mood and heart of fire once more,
For all the gold the world might hold I'd never quit your shore,
I'd live content whate'er God sent with neighbours old and gray,
And lay my bones, 'neath churchyard stones, beside you, Galway Bay.

The blessing of a poor old man be with you night and day,
The blessing of a lonely man whose heart will soon be clay;
'Tis all the Heaven I'll ask of God upon my dying day,
My soul to soar for evermore above you, Galway Bay.

Lanigan's Ball

In the town of Athy one Jeremy Lannigan battered away 'til he hadn't a pound
His father he died and made him a man again left him a farm and ten acres of ground
He gave a grand party to friends and relations who didn't forget him when come to the wall
And if you but listen I'll make your eyes glisten at rows and ructions at Lannigan's Ball

Myself to be sure, got free invitation for all the nice boys and girls that I ask
In less than a minute the friends and relations were dancing as merry as bees round a cask
There were lashing of punch and wine for the ladies Potatoes and cake, bacon and tea
There were the Nolan, Dolans, O'Grady's courting the girls and dancing away

They were doing all kinds of nonsensical polkas all around in a whirligig
Julia and I soon banished their nonsense out on the floor for a reel and jig
How the girls all got mad at me danced till they thought the ceilings would fall
I spent six months in Brooks Academy learning to dance for Lannigan's Ball

Six long months I spent in Dublin, six long months doing nothing at all
Six long months I spent in Dublin learning to dance for Lannigan's Ball
She stepped out, I stepped in again, I stepped out and she stepped in again
She stepped out, I stepped in again, learning to dance for Lannigan's Ball

The boys were merry the girls all hearty dancin' around in couples and groups
An accident happened - Terence McCarthy put his right boot through Miss Finnerty's hoops
The creature she fainted and cried, "Milia murder." Called for her brothers and gathered they all
Carmody swore he'd go no further till he got revenge at Lannigan's Ball

Boys oh boys 'tis then there was ructions I got a kick from young Phelim McHugh
I soon replied to his fine introduction kicked him a terrible hullabaloo
Casey the piper was near gettin' strangled they leapt on his pipes, bellows, chanter and all
Boys and girls all got entangled and the put an end to Lannigan's Ball

The Last Rose of Summer

'Tis the last rose of summer,
Left blooming alone;
All her lovely companions
Are faded and gone;
No flower of her kindred,
No rosebud is nigh,
To reflect back her blushes,
Or give sigh for sigh.

I'll not leave thee, thou lone one!
To pine on the stem;
Since the lovely are sleeping,
Go, sleep thou with them.
Thus kindly I scatter,

Thy leaves o'er the bed,
Where thy mates of the garden
Lie scentless and dead.

So soon may I follow,
When friendships decay,
And from Love's shining circle
The gems drop away.
When true hearts lie withered,
And fond ones are flown,
Oh! who would inhabit
This bleak world alone?

The Rising of the Moon

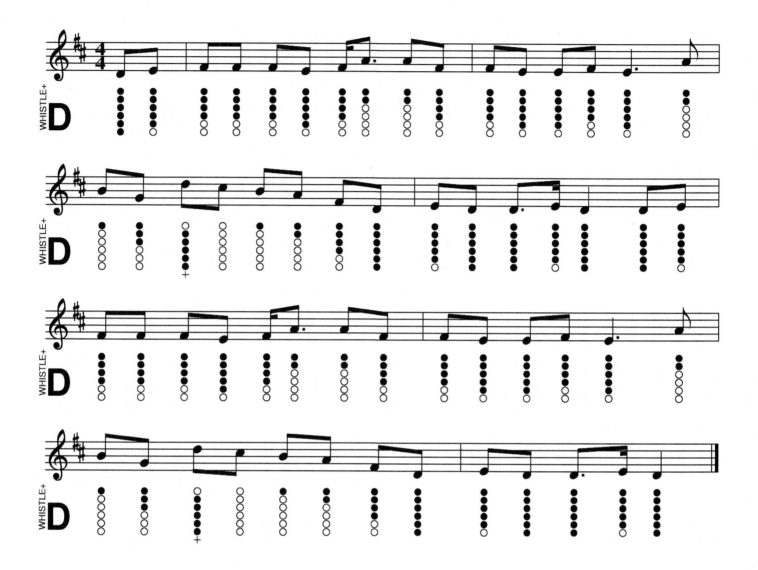

And come tell me Sean O'Farrell tell me why you hurry so
Hush, *a buachaill*, hush and listen and his cheeks were all a glow
I bear orders from the captain get you ready quick and soon
For the pikes must be together by the rising of the moon

By the rising of the moon, by the rising of the moon
For the pikes must be together by the rising of the moon

And come tell me Sean O'Farrell where the gathering is to be
At the old spot by the river quite well known to you and me
One more word for signal token whistle out the marching tune
With your pike upon your shoulder by the rising of the moon

Out from many a mud wall cabin eyes were watching through the night
Many a manly heart was beating for the blessed warning light
Murmurs rang along the valleys to the banshee's lonely croon
And a thousand pikes were flashing by the rising of the moon

All along that singing river that black mass of men was seen
High above their shining weapons flew their own beloved green
Death to every foe and traitor! Whistle out the marching tune
And hurrah, me boys, for freedom, 'tis the rising of the moon

'Tis the rising of the moon, 'tis the rising of the moon
And hurrah, me boys, for freedom, 'tis the rising of the moon

The Lark in the Morning

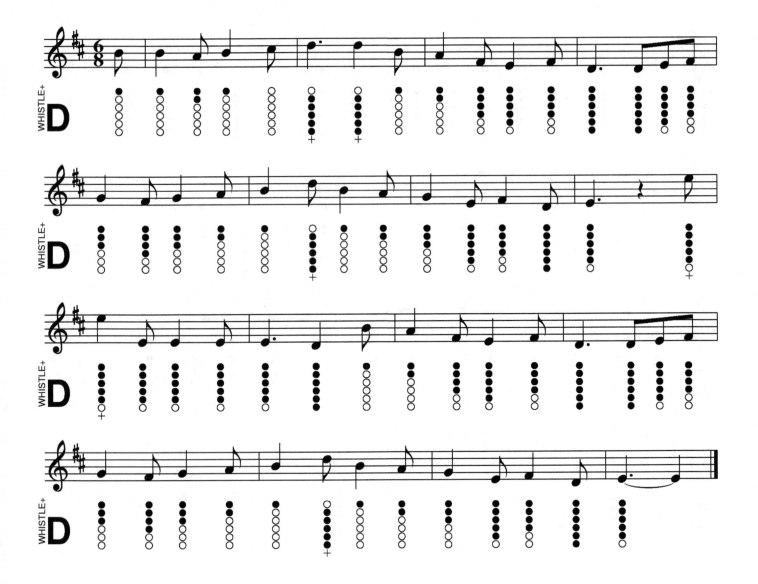

Oh, the lark in the morning she rises off her nest,
She goes off in the air with the dew all on her breast;
And like the jolly ploughboy she whistles and she sings,
She goes home in the evening with the dew all on her wings.

Oh, Roger the ploughboy he is a dashing blade,
He goes whistling and singing all through the leafy glade;
He nests at dark at Susan's, she's handsome, I declare,
She's far more enticing than the birds all in the air.

As they were riding home from the fair all in the town,
Well, the madder was so kissable and the heather was mowed down;
'Twas there they jumped and tumbled all in the new mown hay,
Said, "Take me now or never," this young lass she did say.

When twenty long weeks had all of them gone past,
Well, her mother asked the reason why she thickened 'round the waist;
"It was the jolly ploughboy," this young lass she did say,
"He caused me for to tumble all in the new-mown hay."

So, here's a health to the ploughboy wherever you may be,
Would you like to have a bonnie lass a-sitting on your knee;
With a pint of good strong porter she makes a lovely ring,
She'll make your farmer happier than a prince or a king.

As they were riding home from the fair all in the town,
Well, the madder was so kissable and the heather was mowed down;
'Twas there they jumped and tumbled all in the new mown hay,
Said, "Take me now or never," this young lass she did say.

When twenty long weeks had all of them gone past,
Well, her mother asked the reason why she thickened 'round the waist;
"It was the jolly ploughboy," this young lass she did say,
"He caused me for to tumble all in the new-mown hay."

So, here's a health to the ploughboy wherever you may be,
Would you like to have a bonnie lass a-sitting on your knee;
With a pint of good strong porter she makes a lovely ring,
She'll make your farmer happier than a prince or a king.

A Bunch of Thyme

Come all ye maidens young and fair
And you that are blooming in your prime
Always beware and keep your garden fair
Let no man steal away your thyme

For thyme it is a precious thing
And thyme brings all things to my mind
Thyme with all its flavours, along with all its joys
Thyme, brings all things to my mind

Once I had a bunch of thyme
I thought it never would decay
Then came a lusty sailor who chanced to pass my way
And stole my bunch of thyme away

The sailor gave to me a rose
A rose that never would decay
He gave it to me to keep me reminded
Of when he stole my thyme away

The Leaving of Liverpool

Farewell to you my own true love
I am going far away
I am bound for California
But I know that I'll return some day

So fare thee well, my own true love
And when I return, united we will be
It's not the leaving of Liverpool that grieves me
But, my darling, when I think of thee

I have sailed on a yankee sailing ship
Davy Crockett is her name
And Burgess is the captain of her
And they say she is a floating shame

I have sailed with Burgess once before
And I think I know him right well
If a man is a sailor, he can get along
But if not than he's surely in hell

Oh, the fog is on the harbour love
And I wish I could remain
But I know it will be some long time
Before I see you again

THE BLACK VELVET BAND

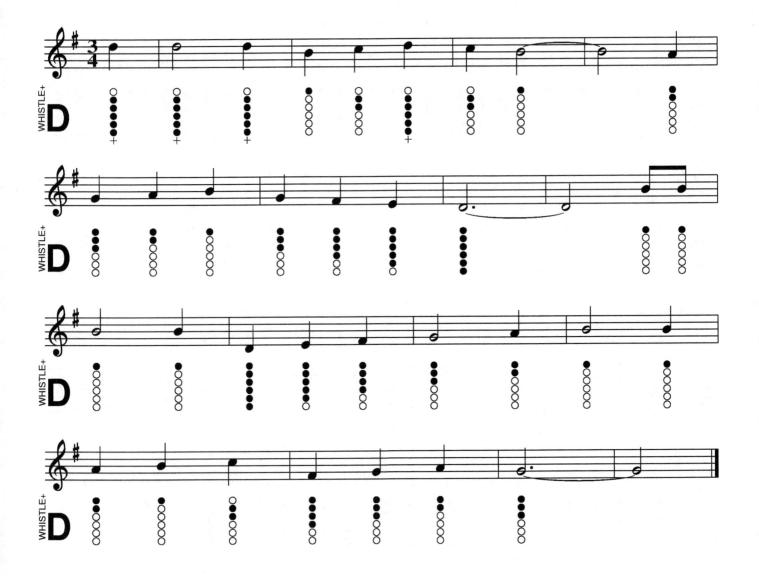

Well, in a neat little town they call Belfast, apprentice to trade I was bound
Many an hours sweet happiness, have I spent in that neat little town
A sad misfortune came over me, which caused me to stray from the land
Far away from my friends and relations, betrayed by the black velvet band

Her eyes they shone like diamonds
I thought her the queen of the land
And her hair it hung over her shoulder
Tied up with a black velvet band

I took a stroll down Broadway, meaning not long for to stay
When who should I meet but this pretty fair maid comes a tripping along the highway
She was both fair and handsome, her neck it was just like a swans
And her hair it hung over her shoulder, tied up with a black velvet band

I took a stroll with this pretty fair maid, and a gentleman passing us by
Well I knew she meant the doing of him, by the look in her roguish black eye
A gold watch she took from his pocket and placed it right in to my hand
And the very first thing that I said was bad luck to the black velvet band

Before the judge and the jury, next morning I had to appear
The judge he says to me: "Young man, your case it is proven clear
We'll give you seven years penal servitude, to be spent far away from the land
Far away from your friends and companions, betrayed by the black velvet band"

So come all you jolly young fellows a warning take by me
When you are out on the town me lads, beware of them pretty colleens
For they feed you with strong drink, until you are unable to stand
And the very next thing that you'll know is you've landed in Van Diemen's Land

Whiskey in the Jar

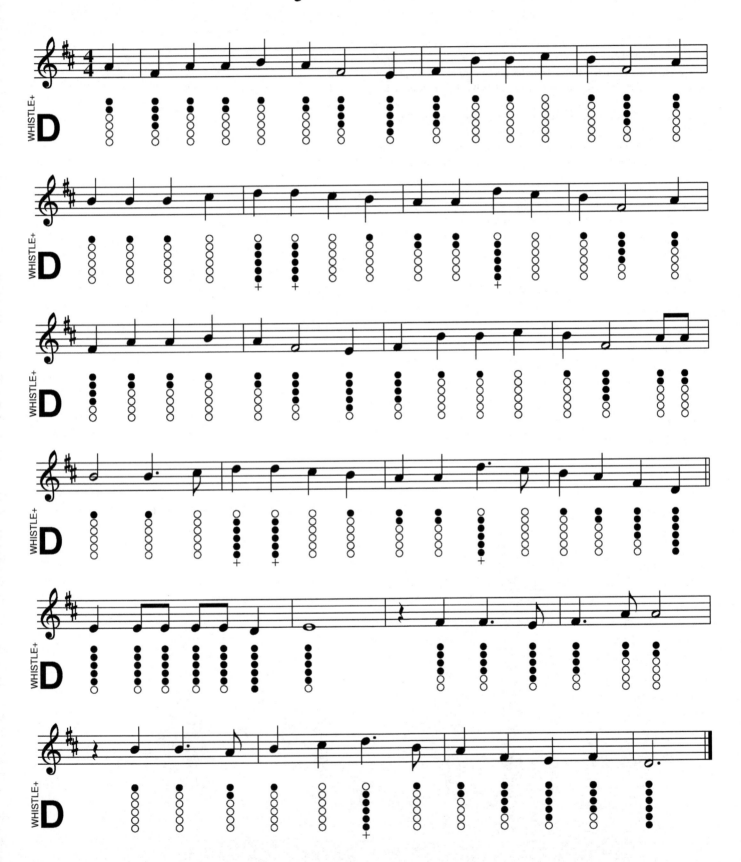

As I was a going over the far famed Kerry mountains
I met with captain Farrell and his money he was counting
I first produced my pistol and I then produced my rapier
Saying "Stand and deliver for you are a bold deceiver"

With me ring dum a doo-dle um dah,
Whack fol the dad-dy o,
Whack fol the dad-dy o,
There's whiskey in the jar

I counted out his money and it made a pretty penny
I put it in me pocket and I took it home to Jenny
She sighed and she swore that she never would deceive me
But the devil take the women for they never can be easy

I went up to my chamber, all for to take a slumber
I dreamt of gold and jewels and for sure 't was no wonder
But Jenny drew me charges and she filled them up with water
Then sent for captain Farrell to be ready for the slaughter

'Twas early in the morning, just before I rose to travel
Up comes a band of footmen and likewise captain Farrell
I first produced me pistol for she stole away me rapier
I couldn't shoot the water, so a prisoner I was taken

Now there's some take delight in the carriages a rolling
and others take delight in the hurling and the bowling
but I take delight in the juice of the barley
and courting pretty fair maids in the morning bright and early

If anyone can aid me 'tis my brother in the army
If I can find his station in Cork or in Killarney
And if he'll go with me, we'll go roving through Killkenny
And I'm sure he'll treat me better than my own a-sporting Jenny

Down by the Glenside

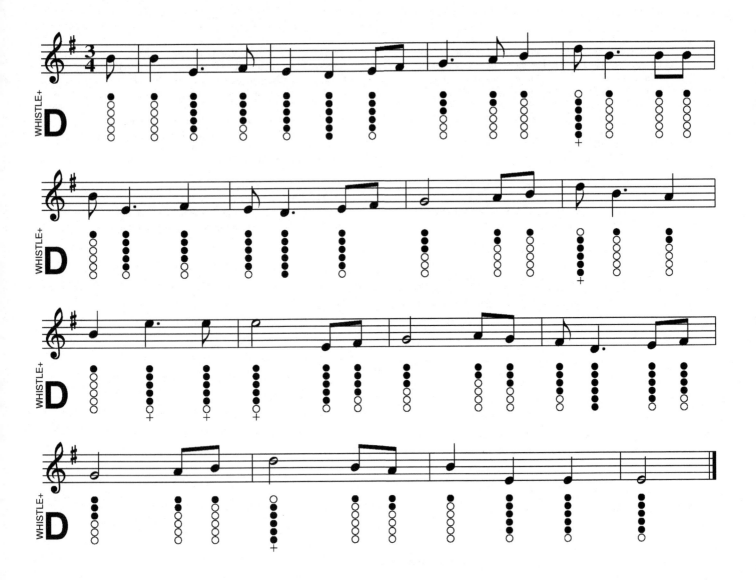

'Twas down by the glenside, I met an old woman
She was picking young nettles and she scarce saw me coming
I listened a while to the song she was humming
Glory O, Glory O, to the bold Fenian men

'Tis fifty long years since I saw the moon beaming
On strong manly forms and their eyes with hope gleaming
I see them again, sure, in all my daydreaming
Glory O, Glory O, to the bold Fenian men.

When I was a young girl, their marching and drilling
Awoke in the glenside sounds awesome and thrilling
They loved poor old Ireland and to die they were willing
Glory O, Glory O, to the bold Fenian men.

Some died on the glenside, some died near a stranger
And wise men have told us that their cause was a failure
They fought for old Ireland and they never feared danger
Glory O, Glory O, to the bold Fenian men

I passed on my way, God be praised that I met her
Be life long or short, sure I'll never forget her
We may have brave men, but we'll never have better
Glory O, Glory O, to the bold Fenian men

WEILE WAILE

There was an old woman and she lived in the woods…
She had a penknife long and sharp…
She stuck the penknife in the baby's heart…
Three policemen came knocking on the door…
Are you the woman that killed the child …

The rope was pulled and she got hung…
And that was the end of the woman in the woods,
A weile weile waile
And that was the end of the baby too
 Down by the river Saile

Part 2 - Irish Gaelic Songs

An bhfaca tú mo Shéamaisín?

An bhfaca tú mo Shéamaisín
Mo Stóirín óg, mo bhuachaillín?
An bhfaca tú mo Shéamaisín
Is é 'dhul síos a' bóthar?

Níl bróg ar bith ar a dhá choisín
Ar a dhá choisín, ar a dhá choisín.
Níl bróg ar bith ar a dhá choisín
Ná caipí air ná clóca

A' dhul ar scoil tá Séamaisín
Mo mhaicín óg, mo bhuachaillín.
A' dhul ar scoil tá Séamaisín
'S a leabhairín bui 'na phóca.

Ar a dhroim tá máilín beag
Tá máilín beag, tá máilín beag.
Ar a dhroim tá máilín beag
'S a lóinín ann is dócha.

An cailín rua

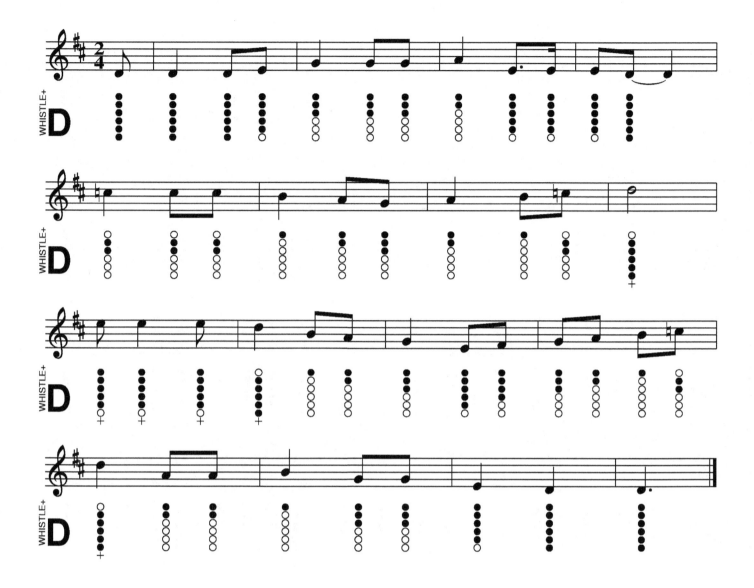

Nach doiligh domhsa mo chailín a mholadh,
Ní hé amháin mar bhí sí rua,
Bhí sí mar gha gréine ag dul in éadan na ngloiní,
Is bhí scéimh mhná na Finne le mo chailín rua.

Thug mé lion í ó bhaile go baile,
Ó Gheaftaí Dhoire go Baile Átha Luain,
Chun fhuil aon mhíle dár shiúil mé ar an fad sin,
Nach dtug mé deoch leanna do mo chailín rua.

B'fhearr liom í ná bó is ná bearrach,
Nó a bhfuil de loingis ag tarraingt chun cuain,
B'fhearr liom arís na cíos Chluain Meala,
Go mbeinn is mo chailín i mBaile Átha Luain.

Chuir mé mo chailín go margadh Shligigh,
Ba é sin féin an margadh bhí daor,
Bhí scilling agus punt ar an mheánpheicín ime,
Is go dtug mé sin le fuinneamh do mo chailín rua.

Chuaigh sí siar agus bróga breac' uirthi,
Ribíní glasuaithne teannta ar a gruaig,
D'éalaigh sí uaimse le buachaill an tsiopa,
Is a Rí nár dheas í, mo chailín rua.

An seanduine dóite

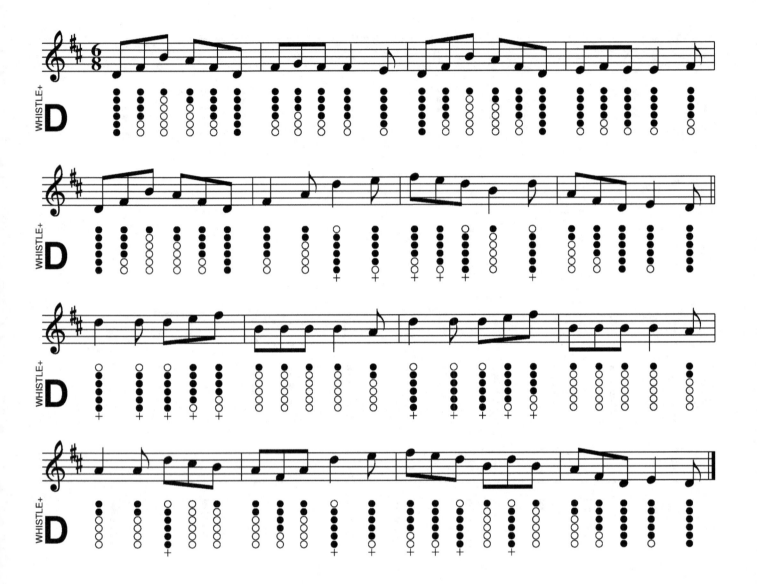

Chuir mé mo sheanduine
Isteach ins an choirnéal
A dhíol bhainne ramhair
Is a dh'ithe aráin eornan,
Dá gcuirfeadh sé a cheann amach
Bhainfinn an tsrón de
Agus d'fhuígfinn an chuid eile
Ag na cailíní óga

Óró, 'sheanduine, 'sheanduine dóite
Is óró, 'sheanduine is mairg a phós thú
Óró, 'sheanduine, 'sheanduine dóite
Luigh ar do leaba is codail do dhóthain

Chuir mé mo sheanduine
Go Sráidbhaile an Róba
Cleite ina hata
Agus búclaí ar a bhróga
Bhí triúir á mhealladh
Is ceathrar á phógadh
Chuala mé i nGaillimh
Gur imigh sé leotha

Báidín Fheilimí

Báidín Fheilimí d'imigh go Gabhla,
Báidín Fheilimí is Feilimí ann.
Báidín Fheilimí d'imigh go Gabhla,
Báidín Fheilimí is Feilimí ann.

Báidín bídeach, báidín beosach,
Báidín bóidheach, báidín Fheilimí
Báidín díreach, báidín deontach
Báidín Fheilimí is Feilimí ann.

Báidín Fheilimí d'imigh go Toraí,
Báidín Fheilimí is Feilimí ann.
Báidín Fheilimí d'imigh go Toraí,
Báidín Fheilimí is Feilimí ann.

Báidín Fheilimí briseadh i dToraí,
Báidín Fheilimí is Feilimí ann.
Báidín Fheilimí briseadh i dToraí,
Báidín Fheilimí is Feilimí ann.

Bean Pháidín

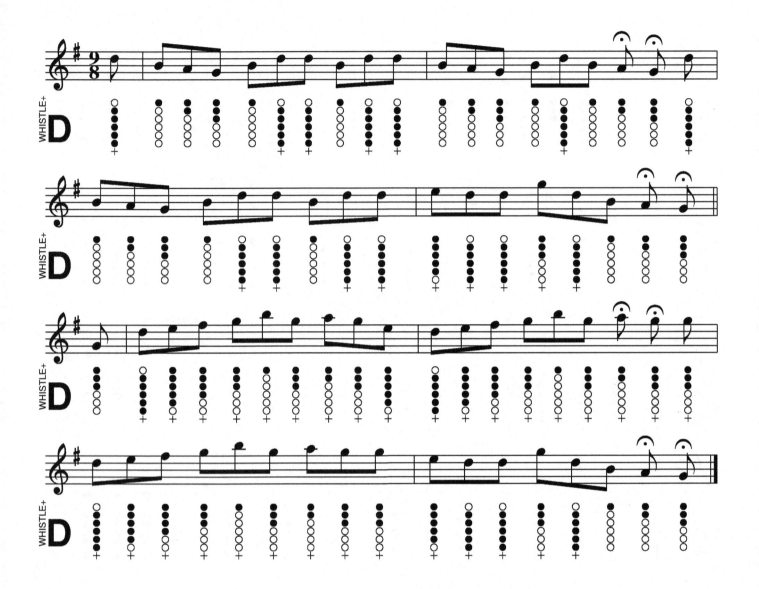

'Sé an trua ghéar nach mise, nach mise
'Sé an trua ghéar nach mise bean Pháidín
'Sé an trua ghéar nach mise, nach mise
Is an bhean atá aige bheith caillte

Rachainn go haonach an Chlocháin
Is siar go Béal Átha na Báighe
Bhreathnoinn isteach tríd an bhfuinneog
Ag súil is go bhfeicfinn bean Pháidín

Rachainn go Gaillimh, go Gaillimh
Is rachainn go Gaillimh le Páidín
Rachainn go Gaillimh, go Gaillimh
Is thiocfainn abhaile sa mbád leis

Go mbristear do chosa, do chosa
Go mbristear do chosa, a bhean Pháidín
Go mbristear do chosa do chosa
Go mbristear do chosa is do chnámha.

Cuaichín Ghleann Néifin

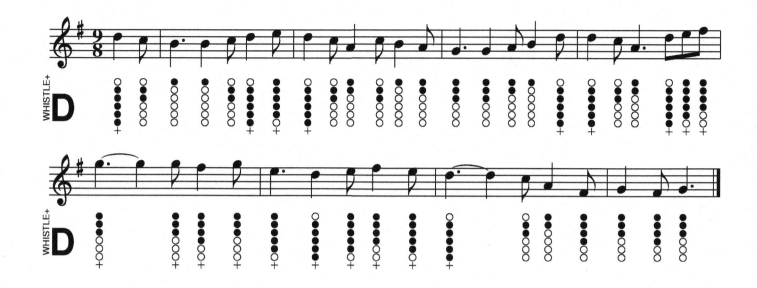

Eireoidh mé amárach le fáinne an lae ghléghil
Agus déanfaidh mé mo dhea-rás amach faoi na sléibhte,
Fagfaidh mé mo bheannacht ag mná deasa an tsaoil seo,
Agus dheamhan an filleadh abhaile dom go labhra an chuach i mbarr na gcraobh ann.

Tá mo ghrá mar bhláth na n-airne a bhíos ag fás i dtús an tsamhraidh,
Nó mar nóiníní bána a bhíos ag snámh ins na gleannta
Nó mar bheadh grian os cionn Carnáin sa tsráid ag dul síos dom,
Is mar siúd a bhios mo ghrá bán ag déanamh ramhailt' tri m'intinn.

Nach aoibhinn don áilléar a mbíonn mo ghrá geal ag dul air,
Nach aoibhinn don talamh a siúlann a bróg air,
Nach ró-aoibhinn don ógfhear a gheobhas mo stóirín le pósadh
Is í réalt eolais na maidine í agus drúcht an tráthnona

CILL CHÁIS

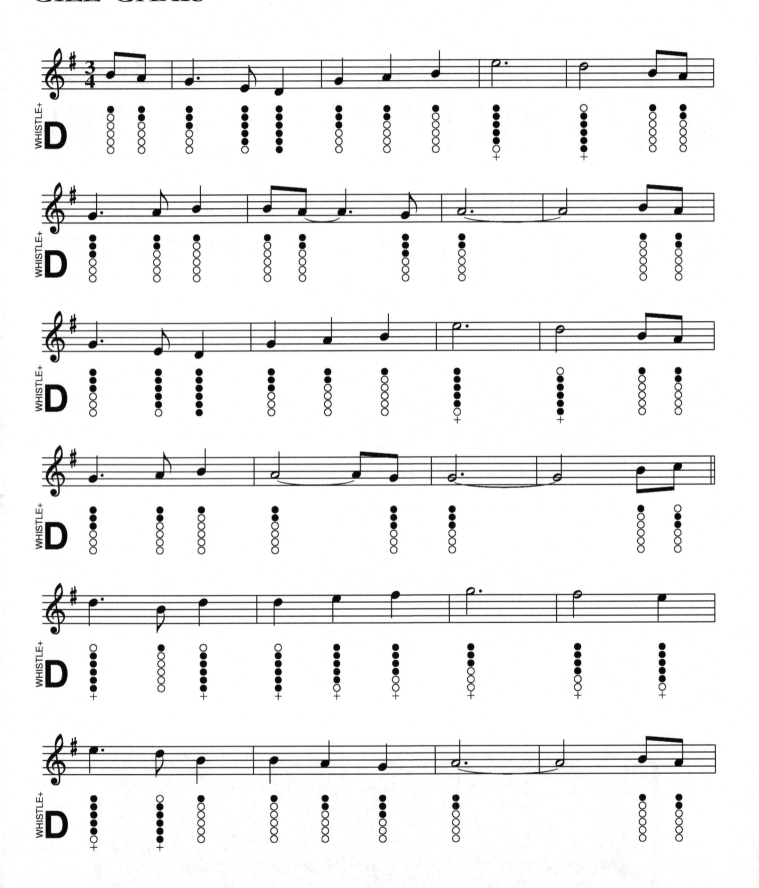

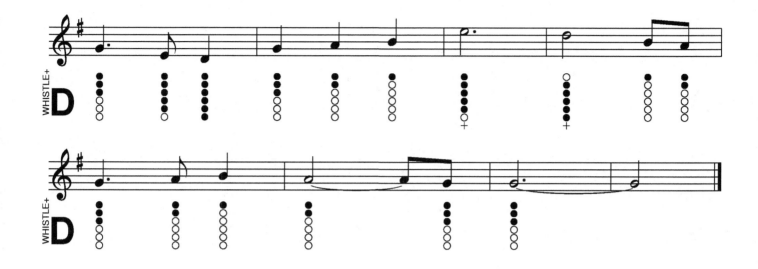

Cad a dhéanfaimid feasta gan adhmad?
Tá deireadh na gcoillte ar lár;
Níl trácht ar Chill Cháis ná ar a teaghlach
Is ní chluinfear a cling go bráth.
An áit úd a gcónaíodh an deighbhean
'Fuair gradam is meidhir thar mhná,
Bhíodh iarlaí ag tarraingt thar toinn ann
I²s an t-aifreann binn á rá.

Ní chluinim fuaim lachan ná gé ann,
Ná fiolar ag éamh cois cuain,
Ná fiú na mbeacha chun saothair
A thabharfadh mil agus céir don slua.
Níl ceol binn milis na n-éan ann
Le hamharc an lae a dhul uainn,
Ná an chuaichín i mbarra na ngcraobh ann,
ós í chuirfeadh an saol chun suain.

Aicim ar Mhuire is ar Íosa
Go dtaga sí arís chughainn slán,
Go mbeidh rincí fada ag dul timpeall,
Ceol fidilí is tinte cnámh;

Go dtógtar an baile seo ár sinsear
Cill Chais bhreá arís go hard,
Is go brách nó go dtiocfaidh an díle
Nach bhfeicfear é arís ar lár.

ÉAMONN AN CHNOIC

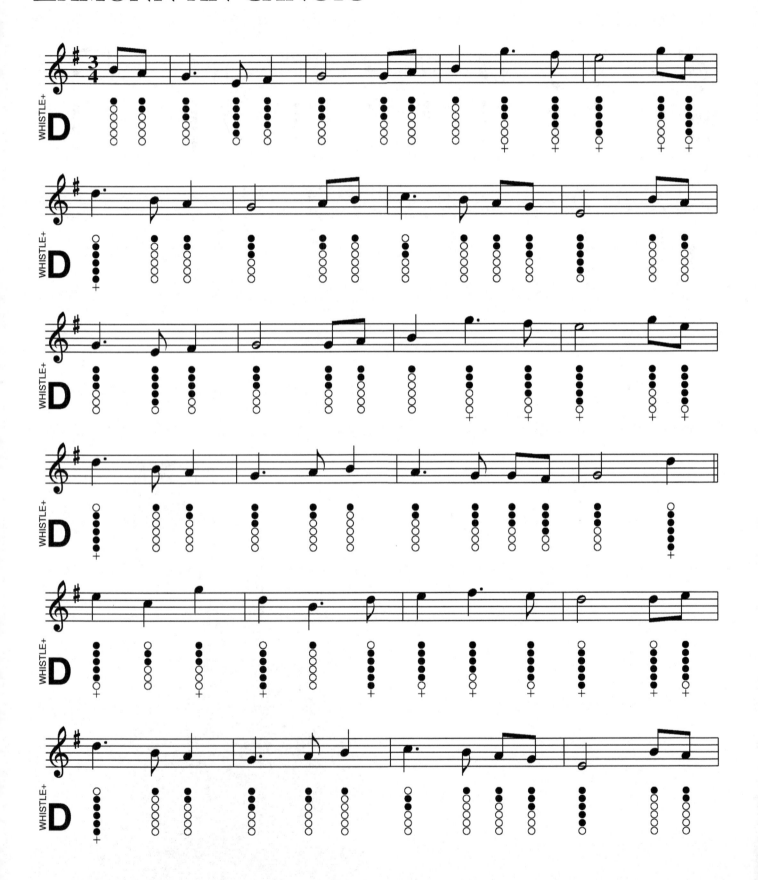

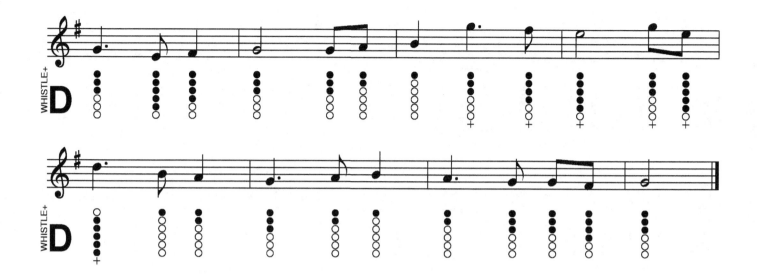

Cé hé sin amu
A bhfuil faobhar a ghuth,
Ag réabadh mo dhorais dhúnta?
Mise Éamonn a' Chnoic,
Atá báite fuar fliuch,
ó shíorshiúl sléibhte is gleannta.

A lao dhil is a chuid,
Cad a dheánfainnse dhuit
Mura gcuirfinn ort binn de mo ghúna?
Is go mbeidh púdar go tiubh
Á shíorshéideagh leat,
Is go mbeimis araon múchta!
Is fada mise amuigh
Faoi shneachta is faoi shioc,
Is gan dánacht agam ar éinne.
Mo sheisreach gan scor,
Mo bhranar gan scor,
Is gan iad agam ar aon chor!
Níl cara agam

Is danaid liom sin
A ghlacfadh mé moch ná déanach.
Is go gcaithfidh mé dul
Thar fairraige soir,
Ó's ann nach bhfuil mo ghaolta.

Cúnla

Cé hé siúd thíos 'tá ag leagadh na gclaíochaí?
Cé hé siúd thíos 'tá ag leagadh na gclaíochaí?
Cé hé siúd thíos 'tá ag leagadh na gclaíochaí?
"Mise mé féin" a deir Cúnnla.

A Chúnla a chroí ná tar níos goire dhom!
A Chúnla a chroí ná tar níos goire dhom!
A Chúnla a chroí ná tar níos goire dhom!
Go deimhin muise tiocfaidh! a deir Cúnla.

Cé hé siúd thíos 'tá ag buaileadh na fuinneoige?
Cé hé siúd thíos 'tá ag buaileadh na fuinneoige?
Cé hé siúd thíos 'tá ag buaileadh na fuinneoige?
"Mise mé féin" a deir Cúnla.

Cé hé siúd thíos 'tá ag fadú na tine dhom?
Cé hé siúd thíos 'tá ag fadú na tine dhom?
Cé hé siúd thíos 'tá ag fadú na tine dhom?
"Mise mé féin" a deir Cúnla.

Cé hé siúd thíos 'tá a' cur uisce sa gciteal dhom?
Cé hé siúd thíos 'tá a' cur uisce sa gciteal dhom?
Cé hé siúd thíos 'tá a' cur uisce sa gciteal dhom?
"Mise mé féin" a deir Cúnnla.

Cé hé siúd thíos 'tá ag tarraingt na pluide dhíom?
Cé hé siúd thíos 'tá ag tarraingt na pluide dhíom?
Cé hé siúd thíos 'tá ag tarraingt na pluide dhíom?
"Mise mé féin" a deir Cúnnla.

Cé hé siúd thíos 'tá ag tochas mo bhonnachaí?
Cé hé siúd thíos 'tá ag tochas mo bhonnachaí?
Cé hé siúd thíos 'tá ag tochas mo bhonnachaí?
"Mise mé féin" a deir Cúnla.

Jimmy mo mhíle stór

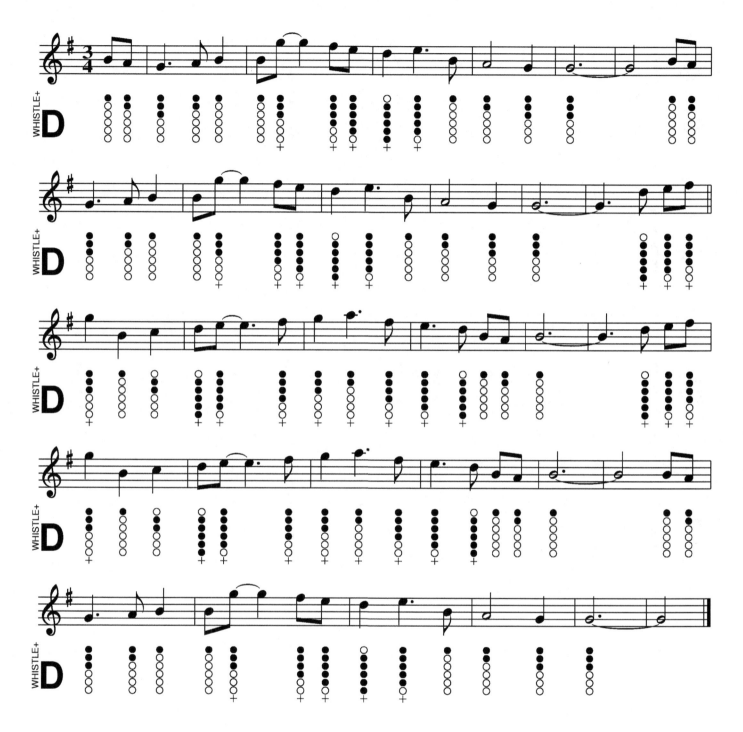

Bliain an taca seo d'imigh uaim rún mo chléibh
Ní thiocfaidh sé abhaile go dtabharfaidh sé cúrsa an tsaoil
Nuair a chífead é rithfead le fuinneamh ró-ard ina chomhair
Agus chlúdód le mil é, is é Jimmy mo mhíle stór.

Bíonn mo mháthair is m'athair ag bearradh's ag bruíon liom féin
Táim giobaithe piocaithe, ciapaithe, cráite dem shaol
Thugas taitneamh don duine úd dob 'fhinne's dob aille snó
Is chuaigh sé ar bhord loinge, is é Jimmy mo mhíle stór

Rachadsa chun coille agus caithféad an chuid eile dem' shaol
San áit ná béidh éinne ag éisteacht le ceol na n-éan
Ag bun an chrainn chaorthainn mar a bhfásann ann féar go leor
Ag tabhart taitnimh don duine úd, is é Jimmy mo mhíle stór

Eibhlín a Rún

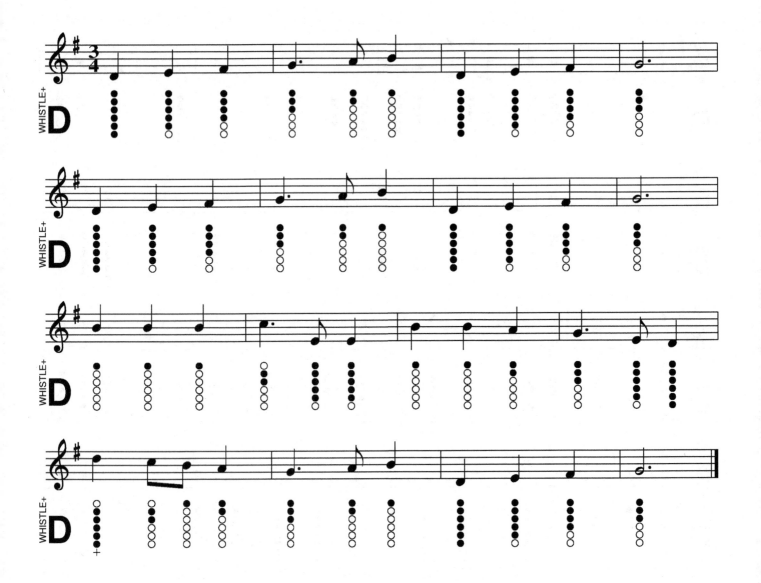

Le grá dhuit níl radharc am cheann,
Eibhlín a Rún,
Is trácht ort is saidhbhreas liom,
Eibhlín a Rún;
Ó mo mhórdháil ró-ghreidhnmhear thú,
sólás na Soillse's tú,
Ó mo lile thú, mo mheidhir is tú,
mo bhruinneal thú go deimhin.
A's mo chlús dá bhfuil sa choill seo's tú.
As mo chroí 'stigh níl leigheas gan tú,
Eibhlín a Rún.

Le cúirtéis na tlúig bhéit, is tú,
Eibhlín a Rún,
Dúrt bréag nú's liam fhéinig tú,
Eibhlín a Rún,
Mar is breátha ná Bhénus tú,
'sis áilne ná'n Réilthean tú;
Ó mo Hélen tú gan bhéim is tú mo rós,
mo lil mo chraobh
Mo stór d'á bhfuil sa tsaol so's tú,
Agus rún mo chroí agus mo chléibh is tú,
Eibhlín a Rún.

ÓRÓ! 'SÉ DO BHEATHA 'BHAILE

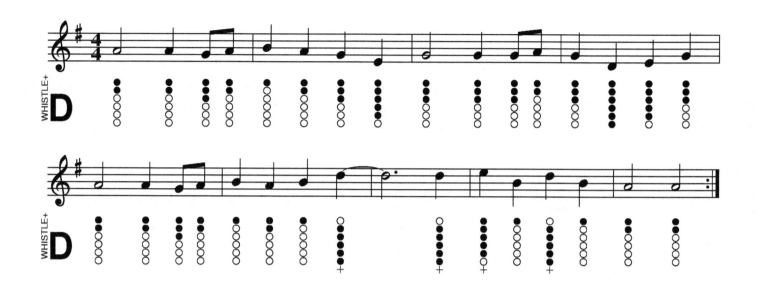

Óró! 'Sé do bheatha 'bhaile
Óró! 'Sé do bheatha 'bhaile
Óró! 'Sé do bheatha 'bhaile
Anois ar theacht an tsamhraidh

'Sé do bheatha a bhean ba léanmhar!
B'é ár gcreach tú bheith i ngéibhinn
Do dhúthaigh bhreá i seilbh meirleach
Is tú díolta leis na Galla

Tá Gráinne Mhaol ag teacht thar sáile
Óglaigh armtha léi mar gharda
Gaeil iad féin is ní Gaill ná Spáinnigh
Is cuirfidh siad ruaig ar Ghalla

A bhuí le Rí na bhFeart go bhfeiceam
Muna mbeinn beo ina dhiaidh ach seachtain
Gráinne Mhaol is míle gaiscíoch
Ag fógairt fáin ar Ghalla

Níl 'na Lá

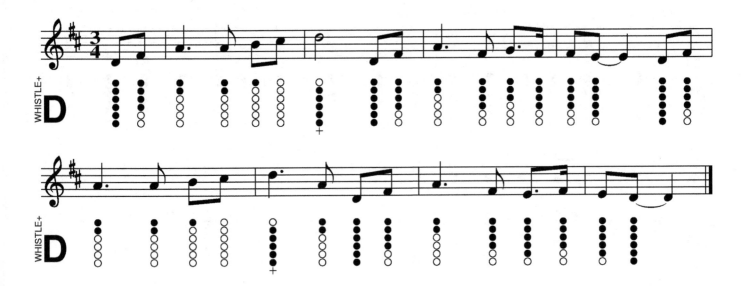

Chuaigh mé 'steach i dteach aréir
Is d'iarr mé cairde ar bhean an leanna;
'Sé dúirt sí liom: "Ní bhfaighidh tú deoir!
Buail an bóthar is gabh abhaile!"

Níl 'na lá, níl, a ghrá;
Níl 'na lá ná baol ar maidin.
Níl 'na lá 's ní bheidh go fóill,
Solas ard atá sa ghealaigh.

Chuir mé féin mo lámh im' phóc'
Is d'iarr mé briseadh corón' uirthi;
'Sé dúirt sí liom: "Buail a' bord
Is bí ag ól anseo go maidin."

Nead na lachan sa mhúta

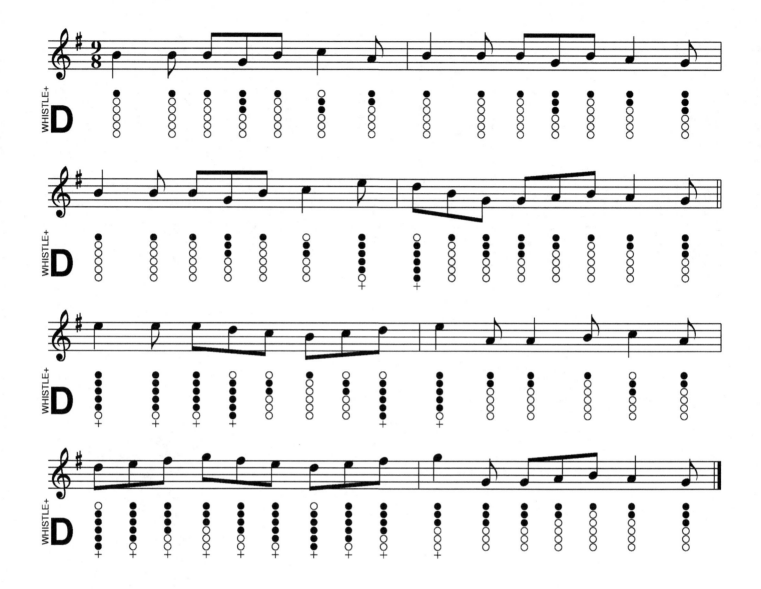

Nead na lachan sa mhúta
Nead na lachan sa mhúta
Nead na lachan sa mhúta
'S cuirfidh mé amach ar an gcuan thú

Haigh dí didil dí didil dí
Haigh dí dídil dí déró
Haigh dí didil dí didil dí
Dídil di didil dí déró

Ceannóidh mé slat agus dorú dhuit
Ceannóidh mé slat agus dorú dhuit
Ceannóidh mé slat agus dorú dhuit
'S cuirfidh mé amach ar an gcuan thú

Siúil a rún

Siúil, siúil, siúil a rún
Siúil go socair agus siúil go ciúin
Siúil go doras agus éalaigh liom
Is go dté tú mo mhúirnín slán

I wish I was on yonder hill
'Tis there I'd sit and cry my fill
And every tear would turn a mill
Is go dté tú mo mhuirnín slán

I'll sell my rock, I'll sell my reel
I'll sell my only spinning wheel
To buy my love a sword of steel
Is go dté tú mo mhúirnín slán

I'll dye my petticoats, I'll dye them red
And round the world I'll beg my bread
Until my parents shall wish me dead
Is go dté tú mo mhúirnín slán

I wish, I wish, I wish in vain
I wish I had my heart again
And vainly think I'd not complain
Is go dté tú mo mhúirnín slán

But now my love has gone to France
To try his fortune to advance
If he e'er comes back 'tis but a chance
Is go dté tú mo mhúirnín slán

Siúbhán Ní Dhuibhir

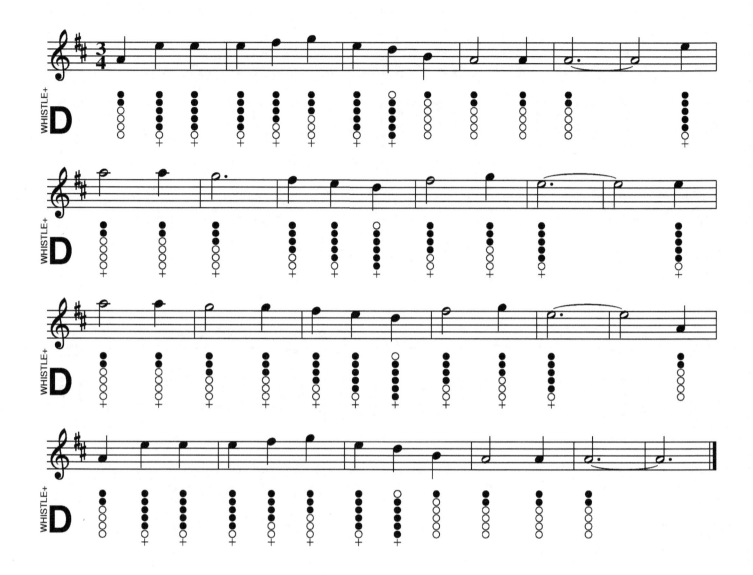

D'éirigh mé ar maidin a tharraint chun aonaigh mhóir
A dhíol is a cheannacht mar a dhéanadh mo dhaoine romham.
Bhuail tart ar an bhealach mé is shuigh mise síos a dh'ól
Is le Siúbhán Ní Dhuibhir gur ól mise luach na mbróg.

A Shiúbháin Ní Dhuibhir, an miste leat mé bheith tinn?
Mo bhrón is mo mhilleadh más miste liom tú bheith i gcill.
Bróinte is muilte bheith 'scileadh ar chúl do chinn
Ach cead a bheith in Iorras go dtara síol Éabha chun cinn.

A Shiúbháin Ní Dhuibhir, is tú bun agus barr mo scéil.
Ar mhná na cruinne go dtug sise an báire léi
Le gile le finne le maise is le dhá dtrian scéimh
Is nach mise an trua Mhuire bheith ag scaradh amárach léi.

A Shiúbháin Ní Dhuibhir, is tú bun agus barr mo scéil.
Ar mhná na cruinne go dtug sise an báire léi
Le gile le finne le maise is le dhá dtrian scéimh
Is nach mise an trua Mhuire bheith ag scaradh amárach léi.

Thiar in Iorras tá searc agus grá mo chléibh,
Planta an leinbh a d'eitigh mo phosadh inné.
Beir scéala uaim chuici má thug mise póg dá béal
Go dtabharfainn dí tuille dá gcuirfeadh sí bólacht léi.

Beir scéala uaim chuige go dearfa nach bpósaim é
Ó chuala mise gur chuir sé le bólacht mé.
Nuair nach bhfuil agamsa maoin nó mórán spré,
Bíodh a rogha bean aige is beidh mise ar mo chomhairle féin.

An Spailpín Fánach

Go deo deo arís ní raghad go Caiseal,
Ag díol ná ag reic mo shláinte,
Ná ar mharagadh na saoire im shuí cois balla,
Im scaoinse ar leataoibh sráide,
Bodairí na tíre ag teacht ar a gcapaill,
Dá fhiafraí an bhfuilim hírálta,
"Ó téanam chun siúil tá an cúrsa fada"
Seo ar siúl an Spailpín Fánach.

Im Spailpín Fánach fágadh mise,
Ag seasadh ar mo shláinte,
Ag siúl an drúchta go moch ar maidin,
'S ag bailiú galair ráithe,
Ní fheicfear corrán im' láimh chun bainte,
Súiste ná feac beag rainne,
Ach bratacha na bhFranncach os cionn mo leapan,
Is píce agam chun sáite.

Mó chúig céad slán chun dúiche m'athar,
'Gus chun an oileáin ghrámhair,
Is chun buachaill na Cúlach os díobh nár mhiste,
In aimsir chasta an ghárda,
Ach anois ó táimse im chadhan bhocht dhealbh,
Imeasc na ndúichí fáin seo,
'Sé mo chumha croí mar fuair mé an ghairm,
Bheith riamh im Spailpín Fánach.

Im Spailpín Fánach fágadh mise,
Ag seasadh ar mo shláinte,
Ag siúl an drúchta go moch ar maidin,
'S ag bailiú galair ráithe,
Ní fheicfear corrán im' láimh chun bainte,
Súiste ná feac beag rainne,
Ach bratacha na bhFranncach os cionn mo leapan,
Is píce agam chun sáite.

Thugamar Féin an Samhradh Linn

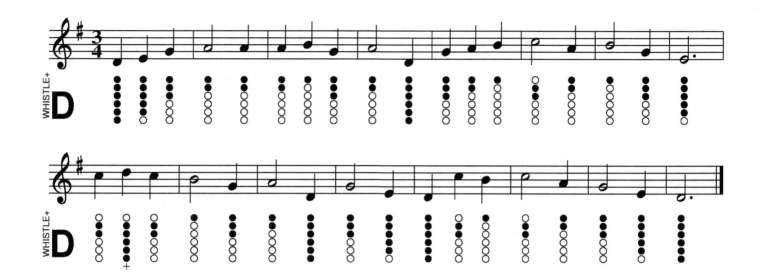

Bábóg na Bealtaine, maighdean an tSamhraidh,
Suas gach cnoc is síos gach gleann,
Cailíní maiseacha bán-gheala gléasta,
Thugamar féin an samhradh linn.

Samhradh, samhradh, bainne na ngamhna,
Thugamar féin an samhradh linn.
Samhradh buí na nóinín glégeal,
Thugamar féin an samhradh linn.

Thugamar linn é ón gcoill chraobhaigh,
Thugamar féin an samhradh linn.
Samhradh buí ó luí na gréine,
Thugamar féin an samhradh linn

Samhradh, samhradh, bainne na ngamhna,
Thugamar féin an samhradh linn.
Samhradh buí na nóinín glégeal,
Thugamar féin an samhradh linn.

Tá an fhuiseog ag seinm is ag luascadh
sna spéartha,
Áthas do lá is bláth ar chrann.
Tá an chuach is an fhuiseog ag seinm le pléisiúr,
Thugamar féin an samhradh linn.

Samhradh, samhradh, bainne na ngamhna,
Thugamar féin an samhradh linn.
Samhradh buí na nóinín glégeal,
Thugamar féin an samhradh linn.

Déirín Dé

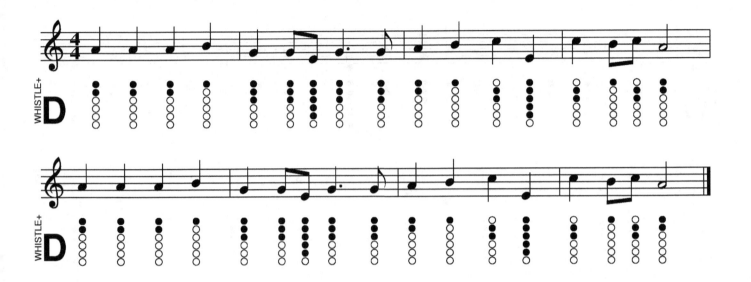

Déirín dé, déirín dé!
Tá'n gabhar donn ag labhairt san bhfraoch,
Déirín dé, déirín dé!
Táid na lachain ag screadaigh san bhféith

Déirín dé, déirín dé!
Geobhaidh ba siar le héirí an lae
Déirín dé, déirín dé!
Is rachaidh mo leanbh dá bhfeighilt ar féar

Déirín dé, déirín dé!
Éireodh gealach is raghaidh grian fé,
Déirín dé, déirín dé!
Is tusa mo leanbh is mo chuid den tsaol

Déirín dé, déirín dé!
Ligfead mo leanbh ag piocadh sméar
Déirín dé, déirín dé!
Ach codladh go sámh go fáinne'n lae

Cailleach an Airgid

'Sí do mhaimeo í, 'sí do mhaimeo í
'Sí do mhaimeo í, 'sí cailleach an airgid
'Sí do mhaimeo í, ó Bhaile Iorrais Mhóir í
'S chuirfeadh sí cóistí
Ar bhóithre Cois Fharraige

Dá bhfeicfeá' an "steam"
'Ghabhail siar Tóin Uí Loin'
'S na rothaí 'ag dul timpeall siar ó na ceathrúnaí
Chaithfeadh sí 'n stiúir naoi n-uair' ar a úl
Is ní choinneodh sí siúl
Le cailleach an airgid

Measann tú an bpósfa', measann tú an bpósfa'
Measann tú an bpósfa', cailleach an airgid?
Tá's a'm nach bpósfadh, tá's agam nach 'pósfadh
Mar tá sé ró-óg agus d'ólfadh sé an t-airgead

Is gairid go bpósfadh, is gairid go bpósfadh
Is gairid go bpósfadh beirt ar an mbaile seo
Is gairid go bpósfadh, is gairid go bpósfadh
Séan Shéamais Mhóir agus Máire Ní
Chathasaigh

An maidrín rua

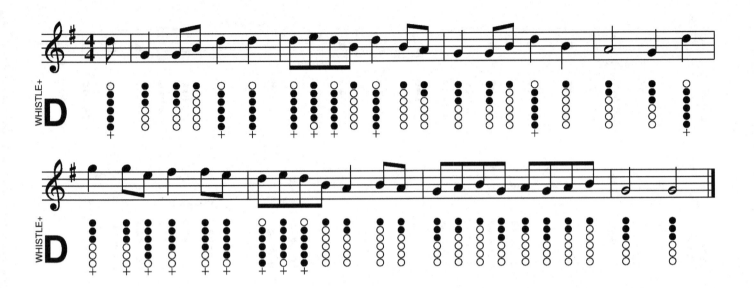

Ag g'bháil ó thuaidh dom thar Shliabh Luachra,
'Gus mise 'cur tuairisc' mo ghéanna,
Ar mo chasadh anuas sea fuair mé a dtuairisc,
Go raibh maidrín rua á n-aoireacht!

An maidrín ru', ru', rua, rua, rua,
An maidrín rua 'tá gránna,
An maidrín rua 'na luí sa luachair,
Agus barr a dhá chluais in airde.

"Good morrow, fox!" "Good morrow, sir!"
"Pray what is that you're eating?"
"A fine fat goose I stole from you
And will you come and taste it?"

"Oh! No indeed, ní áil liom í,
Ní bhlaisfead pioc di ar aon chor,
But I vow and swear you'll dearly pay,
For my fine fat goose you're eating!"

Hark, hark, Finder, Lily agus Piper!
Cruinnigí na gadhair lena chéile
Hark, hark, Truman, is leisce an cú thú
Is maith an cú thú, Bateman!

Tally ho! lena bhonn! Tally ho lena bhonn!
Tally ho! lena bhonn, a choileáinín!
Tally ho! lena bhonn! Tally ho lena bhonn!
Agus barr a dhá chluais in airde!

Greadadh croí cráite ort, a mhaidrín ghránna,
A rug uaim m'ái breá géanna,
Mo choiligh mhóra bhreátha 's mo chearca 'bhí go h-álainn,
Is mo lachain bheaga ab fhearr a bhí in Éirinn!

Trasna na dTonnta

Trasna na dtonnta ' dul siar, ' dul siar!
Slán leis an uaigneas is slán leis an gcian!
Geal é mo chroí agus geal í an ghrian!
Geal bheith ag filleadh go hÉirinn!

Chonac mo dhóthain de thíortha i gcéin,
Ór agus airgead, saibhreas an tsaoil.
Éiríonn an croí 'nam le breacadh gach lae
'S mé 'g druidim le dúthaigh mo mhuintir' agus…

Muintir an iarthair 's iad cairde mo chroí;
Fáilte 'gus fiche beidh romham ar gach taobh;
Ar fhágaint an tsaoil seo 'sé guím ar an rí:
Gur leosan a shínfear i gcré mé agus…

ÓRÓ MO BHÁIDÍN

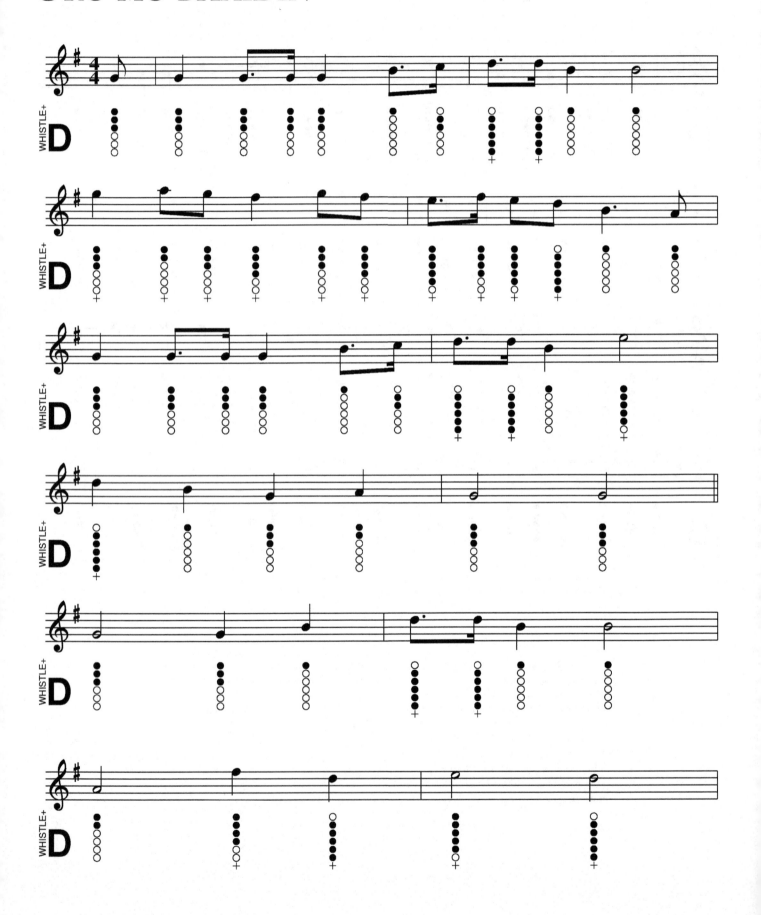

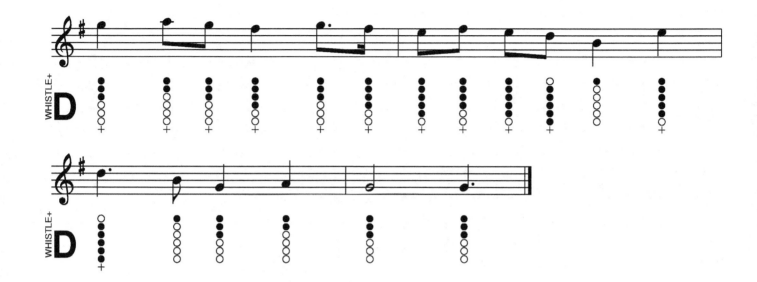

Óró mo bháidín
Ag snámh ar a'gcuan
Óró mo bháidín
Faighimis na máidí
Agus téimis chun siuil
Óró mo bháidín

Óró mo churaichín ó
Óró mo bháidín

Crochfaidh mé seolta
Is rachaidh mé siar
Óró mo bháidín
'S go hOíche Fhéil' Eoin
Ní thiocfaidh mé aniar
Óró mo bháidín

Nach lúfar í ag iomramh
Soir agus siar,
Óró mo churaichín ó,
Asárú ní bhfaighidh tú
Ó Árainn go Cliar,
Óró mo bháidín.

Cailin na gruaige doinne

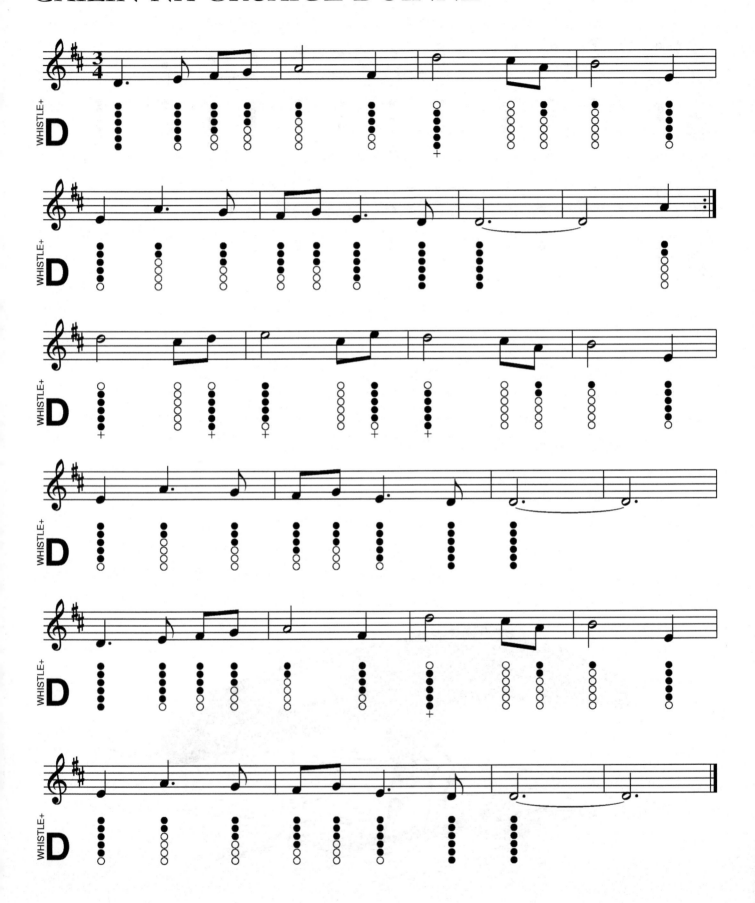

Ar bhantaibh an tSróil sea d'fhagas mo stór,
'S a maithrín ag gleo gan dabht léi.
'D taobh grá ' thabhairt dom shórt sa d'fhánaí gan treoir,
Gan cairne buí óir i gcabhair dom.
'S í an bháb mhiochair modhail [mhodúil] ' chuir bláth ar mo sceol,
'S is páiste bhí óg gan dabht í
'S nach breá deas mo shórt ag geáitseáil ar bord,
Le cailín na gruaige doinne.

Is 'neosfad mo stair dom mhuintir ar fad.
Cé cloíte go lag gan mheabhair mé,
Ag smaoineamh 's ag brath 's ag tnuth len í theacht
Gach oíche 'gus maidin Domhnaigh.
Rince go pras, aoibhneas ná cleas,
Ní smaoiním le heaspa meabhrach,
Ach mo croí istigh a shlad le dian-díograis searc,
Do chailín na gruaige doinne.

Is tréithlag a bhím gan éinne dem bhuíon
Ag déanamh aon suim' sa domhan díom,
'S is baolach dá dhroim go n-éagfad gan mhoill,
Am éigin ar dith mo mheabhrach,
Le saorghuth a cinn go léimid aníos,
Na héisc as an linn ag leabhaireach,
`S dá bhreáthacht sin mar ní, ní shásódh mo chroí,
Gan cailín na gruaige doinne.

AR ÉIRINN NÍ N-EÓSAINN CÉ H-Í

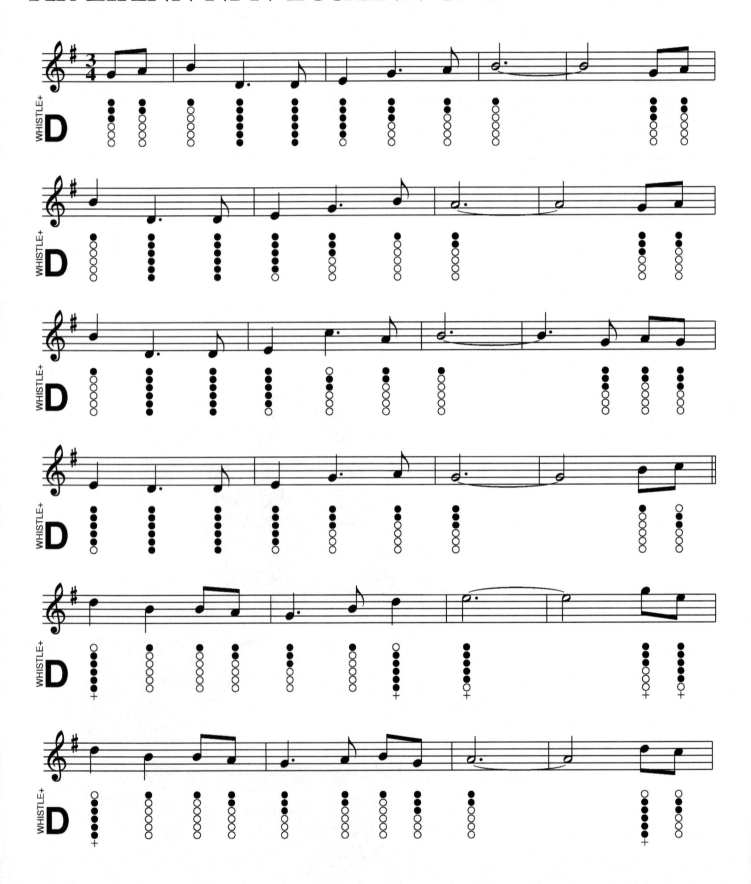

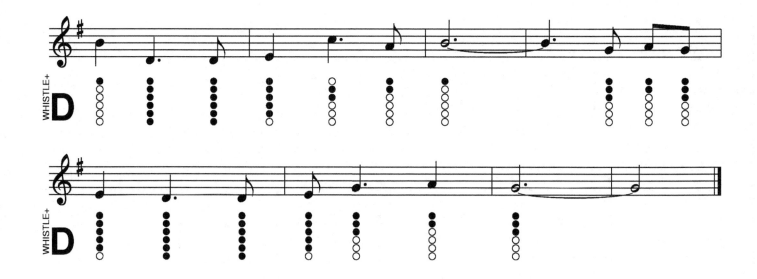

Aréir is mé téarnamh um' neoin
Ar an dtaobh thall den teóra 'na mbím,
Do théarnaig an spéir-bhean im' chómhair
D'fhág taomanach breóite lag sinn.
Do ghéilleas dá méin is dá cló,
Dá béal tanaí beó mhilis binn,
Do léimeas fé dhéin dul 'na cómhair,
Is ar éirinn ní n-eósainn cé h-í.

Dá ngéilleadh an spéir-bhean dom' ghlór,
Siad ráidhte mo bheól a bheadh fíor;
Go deimhin duit go ndéanfainn a gnó
Do léirchur i gcóir is i gcrich.
Dó léighfinn go léir stair dom' stór,
'S ba mhéinn liom í thógaint dom chroí,
'S do bhearfainn an chraobh dhi ina dóid,
Is ar éirinn ní n-eósainn cé h-í.

Tá spéir-bhruinneal mhaordha dheas óg
Ar an taobh thall de'n teóra 'na mbím.
Tá féile 'gus daonnacht is meóin
Is deise ró mhór ins an mhnaoi,
Tá folt lei a' tuitim go feóir,
Go cocánach ómarach buí.
Tá lasadh 'na leacain mar rós,
Is ar éirinn ní n-eósainn cé h-í.

Beidh aonach amárach

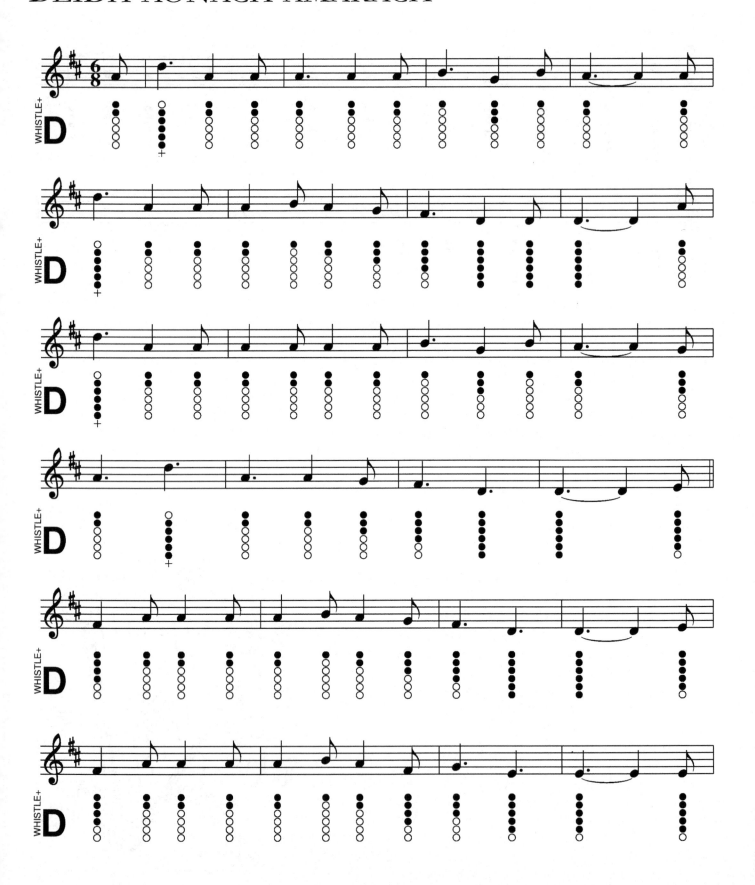

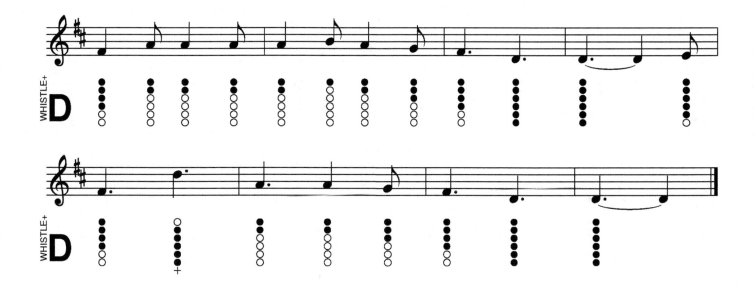

Beidh aonach amárach in gContae an Chláir
Beidh aonach amárach in gContae an Chláir
Beidh aonach amárach in gContae an Chláir
Cén mhaith domh é ní bheidh mé ann

'S a mháithrín, an ligfidh tú chun aonaigh mé?
'S a mháithrín, an ligfidh tú chun aonaigh mé?
'S a mháithrín, an ligfidh tú chun aonaigh mé?
'S a mhuirnín ó ná héiligh é.

Níl tú a deich nó a haon déag fós.
Níl tú a deich nó a haon déag fós.
Níl tú a deich nó a haon déag fós.
Nuair a bheidh tú trí déag beidh tú mór.

Táim-se i ngrá le gréasaí bróg.
Táim-se i ngrá le gréasaí bróg.
Táim-se i ngrá le gréasaí bróg.
Mur' bhfaigh mé é ní bheidh mé beo.

Bfhearr liom féin mo ghréasaí bróg.
Bfhearr liom féin mo ghréasaí bróg.
Bfhearr liom féin mo ghréasaí bróg.
Á oifigeach airm faoi lásaí óir.

Tá 'níon bheag agam is tá sí óg
Tá 'níon bheag agam is tá sí óg
Tá 'níon bheag agam is tá sí óg
Is tá sí i ngrá leis an ghreasaí bróg

'S iomaí bean a phós go h-óg
'S iomaí bean a phós go h-óg
'S iomaí bean a phós go h-óg
Is a mhair go socair lena greasaí bróg

B'fhearr liom féin mo ghreasaí bróg
B'fhearr liom féin mo ghreasaí bróg
B'fhearr liom féin mo ghreasaí bróg
N fir na n'arm faoina lascú óir

www.tradschool.com

TÁ MÉ I MO SHUÍ

Tá mé i mo shuí ó d'éirigh an ghealach aréir,
Ag cur tine síos go buan is á fadú go géar,
Tá bunadh an tí ina luí is tá mise liom féin,
Tá na coiligh ag glaoch is tá an saol ina gcodladh ach mé.

Sheacht mh'anam déag, do bhéal, do mhalaí is do ghrua,
Do shúil ghorm ghlé gheal faoinar thréig mé aiteas is suairc,
Le cumha i do dhiaidh ní léir dom an bealach a shiúl,
Is a chara mo chléibh, tá an saol ag dul idir mé is tú.

Deireann lucht léinn gur cloíte an galar an grá,
Char admhaigh mé é go ndearna sé mo chroí istigh a chrá,
Aicíd ró-ghéar, faraor nár sheacain mé í,
Chuir sí arraing is céad go géar trí cheartlár mo chroí.

Casadh bean sí dom thíos ag Lios Bhéal an Áth',
D'fhiafraigh mé díthe an scaoilfeadh glas ar bith grá,
Duirt sí os íseal i mbriathra soineanta sámha,
"An grá a theann fan chroí, cha scaoiltear as é go brach."

Buachaill ón Éirne

Buachaill ón Éirne mé
Is bhréagfainn féin cailín deas óg.
Ní iarrfainn bó spré léithe
Tá mé féin saibhir go leor.
Is liom Corcaigh dá mhéid é,
Dhá thaobh an ghleanna is Tír Eoghain.
Is mura n-athraí mé béasaí
Is mé n' t-oidhre ar Chontae Mhaigh Eo.

Rachaidh mé amárach
A dhéanamh leanna fán choill
Gan choite, gan bád,
Gan gráinín brach' ar bith liom
Ach duilliúr na gcraobh
Mar éide leapa os mo chionn
Is óró a sheacht m'anam déag thú
Is tú ag féachaint orm anall.

Buachailleacht bó, mo lao,
Nár chleacht mise ariamh
Ach ag imirt is ag ól
Le hógmhná deasa fá shliabh.
Má chaill mé mo stór
Ní móide gur chaill mé mo chiall
Is ní mó liom do phóg
Ná an bhróg atá ar caitheamh le bliain.

A chuisle is a stór
Ná pós an seanduine liath
Ach pós an fear óg, mo lao,
Mura maire sé ach bliain
Nó beidh tú go fóill
Gan ó nó mac os do chionn
A shilfeadh an deor
Tráthnóna nó ar maidin go trom.

Dúlamán na binne buí

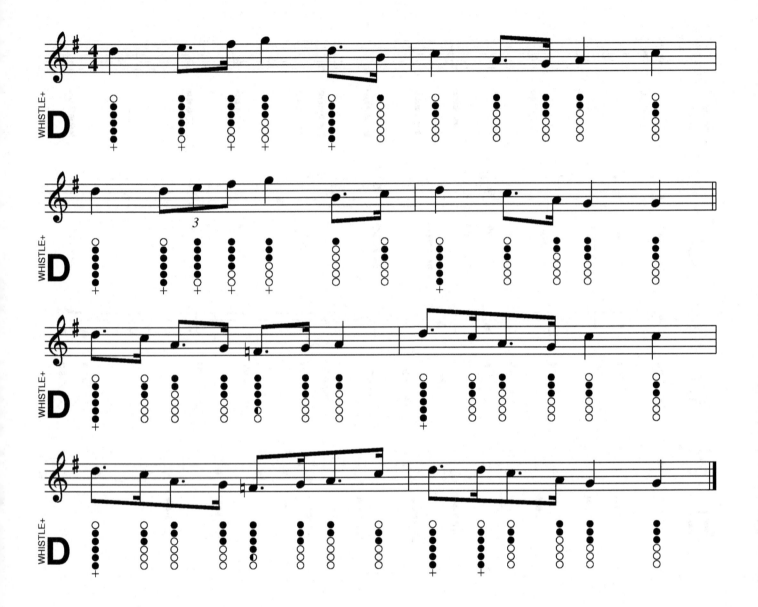

A'níon mhín ó
Sin anall na fir shúirí
A mháithair mhín ó
Cuir na roithléan go dtí mé

Dúlamán na binne buí
Dúlamán Gaelach
Dúlamán na binne buí
Dúlamán Gaelach

Tá ceann buí óir
Ar an dúlamán gaelach
Tá dhá chluais mhaol
Ar an dúlamán gaelach

Rachaimid 'un an Iúr
Leis an dúlamán gaelach
Ceannóimid bróga daora
Ar an dúlamán gaelach

Bróga breaca dubha
Ar an dúlamán gaelach
Tá bearéad agus triús
Ar an dúlamán gaelach

Ó chuir mé scéala chuici
Go gceannóinn cíor dí
'Sé an scéal a chuir sí chugam
Go raibh a ceann cíortha
Caidé thug tú 'na tíre?

Arsa an dúlamán gaelach
Ag súirí le do níon
Arsa an dúlamán maorach

Chan fhaigheann tú mo 'níon
Arsa an dúlamán gaelach
Bheul, fuadóidh mé liom í
Arsa an dúlamán maorach

Dúlamán na binne buí
Dúlamán a' tsleibhe
Dúlamán na farraige
Is dúlamán a' deididh

Bheir mé ó

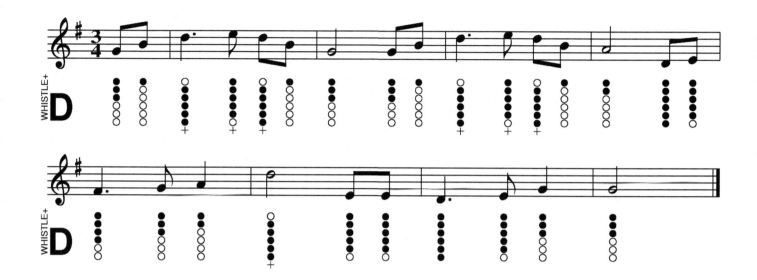

Bheir mí óró, bhean ó
Bheir mí óró, ó bhean í
Bheir mí óró ó hó
Tá mé brónach is tú i m'dhith

Is iomaí oíche fliuch is fuar
Thug mé cuairt is mé liom féin
Nó go tháinig mé san áit
Mar a raibh grá geal mó chléibh

I mo chláirseach ní raibh ceol
I mo mheoraibh ní raibh brí
Nó gur luaigh tú do rún
Is fuair mé eolas ar mo dhán

Part 3 - Scottish Folk Songs

Gin I Were

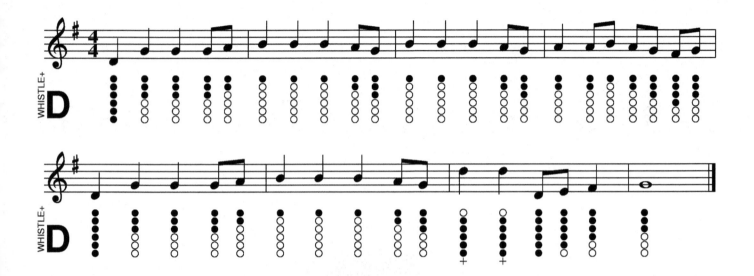

Gin I were whaur the gaudie rins
Whaur the gaudie rins, whaur the gaudie rins
Gin I were whaur the gaudie rins
At the back o' Bennachie

Oh I niver had but twa richt lads
Aye twa richt lads, twa richt bonnie lads
I niver had but twa richt lads
That dearly courted me

And ane was killed at the laurin' fair
The laurin' fair, at the laurin' fair
Oh ane was killed at the laurin' fair
The ither was droont in the Dee

And I gave to him the haunin' fine
The haunin' fine, the haunin' fine
Gave to him the haunin' fine
His mornin' dressed tae be

Well, he gave to me the linen fine
The linen fine, the linen fine
Gave to me the linen fine
Me windin' sheet tae be

Gin I were whaur the gaudie rins
Whaur the gaudie rins, whaur the gaudie rins
Gin I were whaur the gaudie rins
At the back o' Bennachie

Wild Mountain Thyme

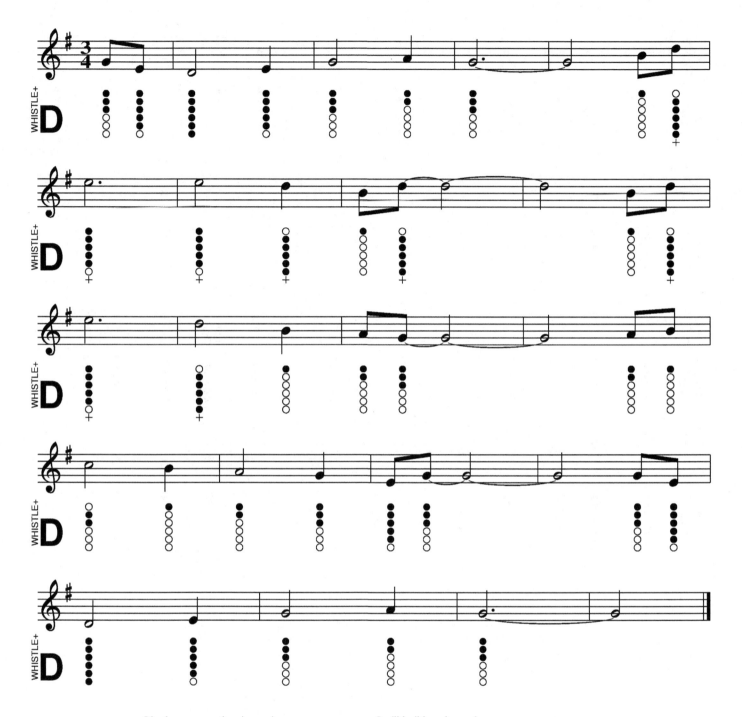

Oh, the summer time is coming,
And the trees are blooming,
And the wild mountain thyme
Grows around the blooming heather.
Will you go, lassie, go?

And we'll all go together
To pull wild mountain thyme
All around the blooming heather,
Will you go, lassie, go?

I will build my love a bower
By yon clear and crystal fountain,
And all around the bower,
I'll pile flowers from the mountain.
Will you go, lassie, go?

If my true love, she won't have me,
I will surely find another
To pull wild mountain thyme
All around the blooming heather.
Will you go, lassie, go?

Scots Wha Hae

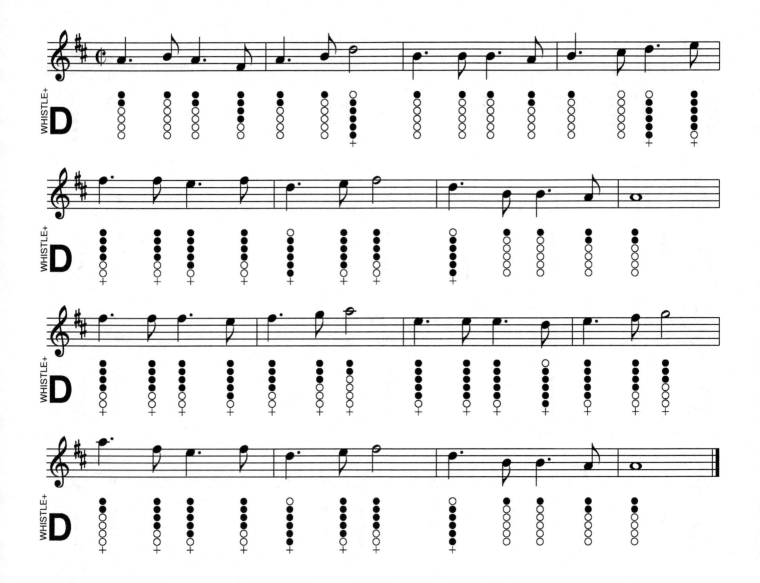

Scots, wha hae wi' Wallace bled,
Scots, wham Bruce has aften led;
Welcome to your gory bed,
Or to victory!

Now's the day, and now's the hour;
See the front o' battle lour;
See approach proud Edward's power—
Chains and slavery!

Wha will be a traitor knave?
Wha can fill a coward's grave!
Wha sae base as be a slave?
Let him turn and flee!

Wha for Scotland's king and law
Freedom's sword will strongly draw,
Freeman stand, or freeman fa',
Let him follow me!

By oppression's woes and pains!
By your sons in servile chains!
We will drain our dearest veins,
But they shall be free!

Lay the proud usurpers low!
Tyrants fall in every foe!
Liberty's in every blow!—
Let us do or die! .

Ye Banks and Braes

Ye banks and braes o' bonnie Doon
How ye can bloom so fresh and fair
How can ye chant ye little birds
And I sae weary fu' o' care

Ye'll break my heart ye warbling birds
That wantons thro' the flowering thorn
Ye mind me o' departed joys
Departed never to return

Oft hae I rov'd by bonnie Doon
To see the rose and woodbine twine
And ilka bird sang o' its love
And fondly sae did I o' mine

Wi' lightsome heart I pu'd a rose
Fu' sweet upon its thorny tree
But my false lover stole my rose
But ah! She left the thorn wi' me

My Bonnie Lies Over the Ocean

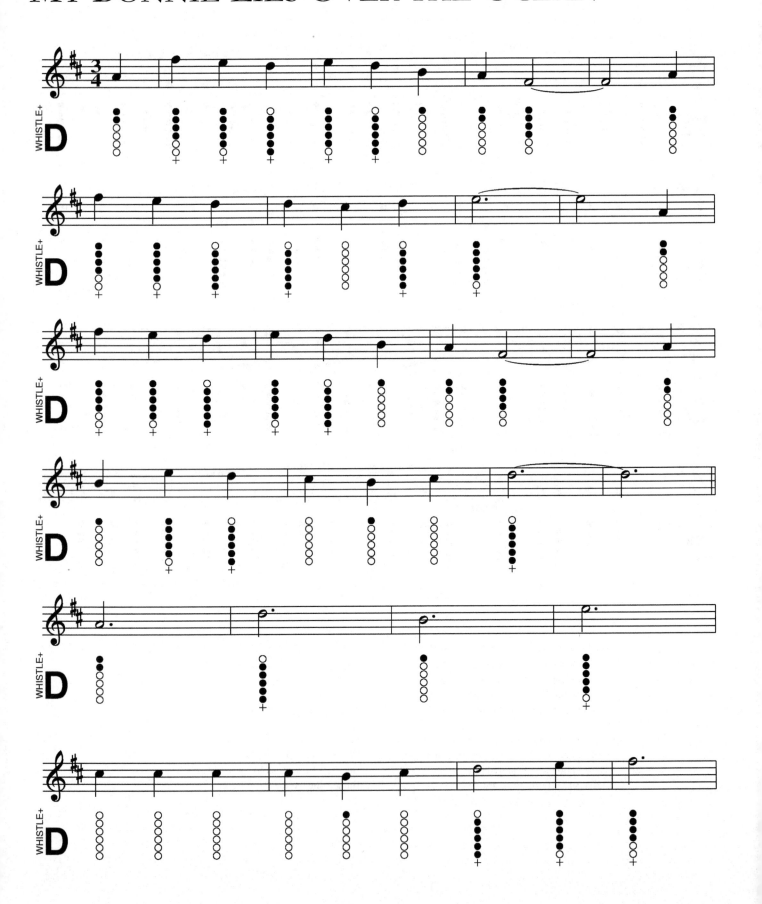

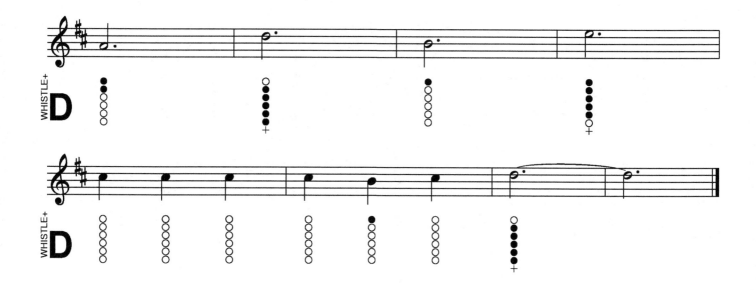

My Bonnie lies over the ocean	Oh blow the winds over the ocean
My Bonnie lies over the sea	And blow the winds over the sea
My Bonnie lies over the ocean	Oh blow the winds over the ocean
Oh, bring back my Bonnie to me...	And bring back my Bonnie to me

My Bonnie lies over the ocean
My Bonnie lies over the sea
My Bonnie lies over the ocean
Oh, bring back my Bonnie to me...

Bring back, bring back
Bring back my Bonnie to me, to me
Bring back, bring back
Bring back my Bonnie to me

Last night as I lay on my pillow
Last night as I lay on my bed
Last night as I lay on my pillow
I dreamt that my Bonnie was dead

Oh blow the winds over the ocean
And blow the winds over the sea
Oh blow the winds over the ocean
And bring back my Bonnie to me

Bring back, bring back
Bring back my Bonnie to me, to me
Bring back, bring back
Bring back my Bonnie to me

The winds have blown over the ocean
The winds have blown over the sea
The winds have blown over the ocean
And brought back my Bonnie to me

Coming Through the Rye

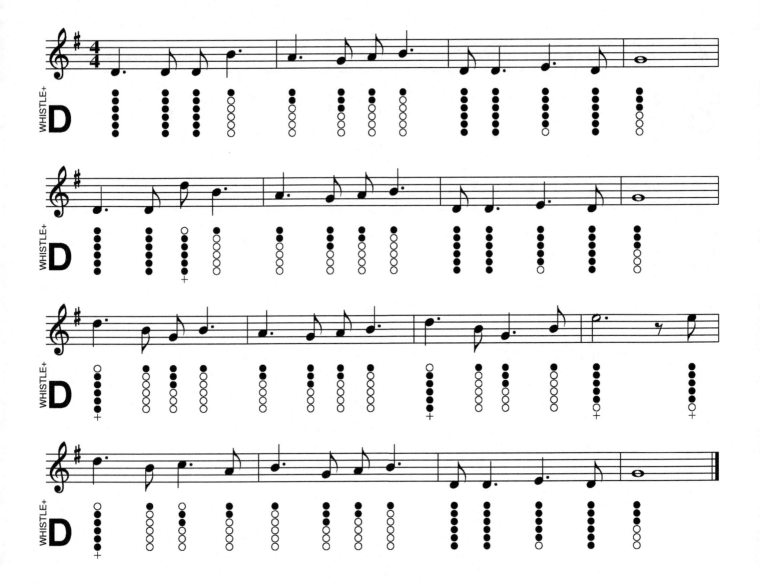

Gin a body meet a body,
Comin' through the rye
Gin a body kiss a body,
Need a body cry?
Ilka lassie has a laddie
Nane, they say, ha'e I
Yet a' the lads they smile at me
When comin' through the rye

Gin a body meet a body,
Comin' frae the well,
Gin a body kiss a body,
Need a body tell?
Ilka lassie has a laddie,
Nane, they say, ha'e I,
But all the lads they smile at me
When coming though the rye.

Gin a body meet a body
Comin' frae the town,
Gin a body meet a body,
Need a body frown?
Ilka lassie has a laddie,
Nane, they say, ha'e I,
But all the lads they lo'e me weel
And what the waur am I?

Amang the train there is a swain
I dearly lo'e mysel'
But whaur his hame or what his name,
I dinna care to tell.
Ilka lassie has a laddie,
Nane, they say, ha'e I,
But all the lads they lo'e me weel
And what the waur am I?

Green Grow the Rashes O

Green grow the rashes , O;
Green grow the rashes , O;
The sweetest hours that e'er I spend,
Are spent amang the lasses, O.

There's nought but care on ev'ry han' ,
In ev'ry hour that passes, O:
What signifies the life o' man,
An' 'twere na for the lasses, O.

Katie Bairdie

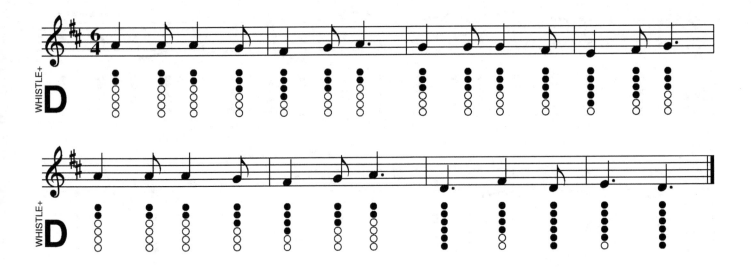

Katie Bairdie had a coo
Black and white aboot the moo
Wisn't that a dainty coo?
Dance Katie Bairdie

Katie Bairdie had a hen
Toddled but and toddled ben
Wisn't that a dainty hen?
Dance Katie Bairdie

Katie Bairdie had a pig
It could dance the Irish jig
Wisn't that a funny pig?
Dance Katie Bairdie

Katie Bairdie had a wean
Widnae play oot in the rain
Wisn't that a clever wean?
Dance Katie Bairdie

Loch Lomond

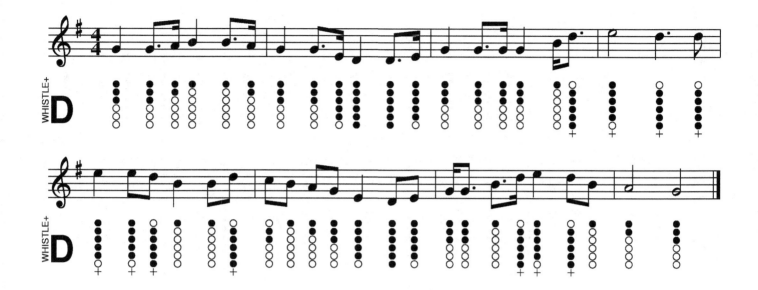

By yon bonnie banks and by yon bonnie braes
Where the sun shines bright on Loch Lomond
Where me and my true love will never meet again
On the bonnie, bonnie banks of Loch Lomond.

O you'll take the high road, and I'll take the low road
And I'll be in Scotland before ye
For me and my true love will never meet again
On the bonnie, bonnie banks of Loch Lomond.

'Twas there that we parted in yon shady glen
On the steep, steep sides of Ben Lomond
Where in soft purple hue, the highland hills we view
And the moon coming out in the gloaming.

The Campbells are Coming

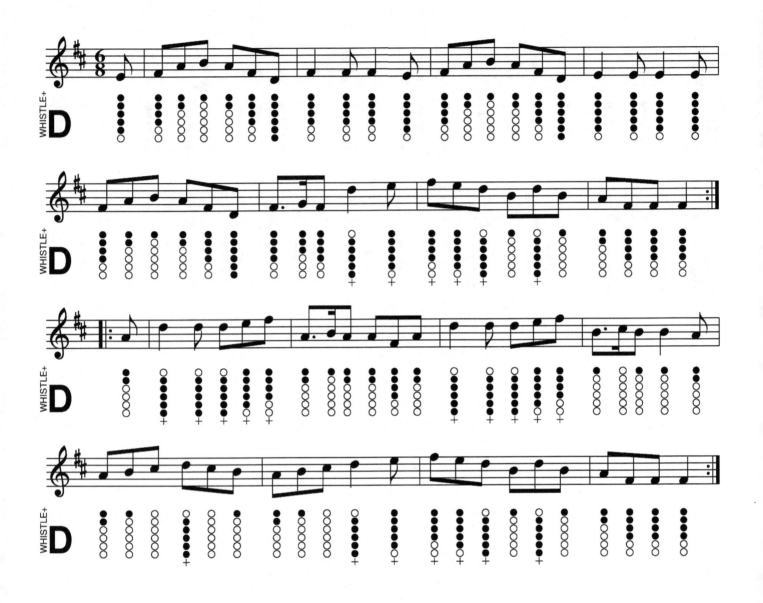

The Calton Weaver

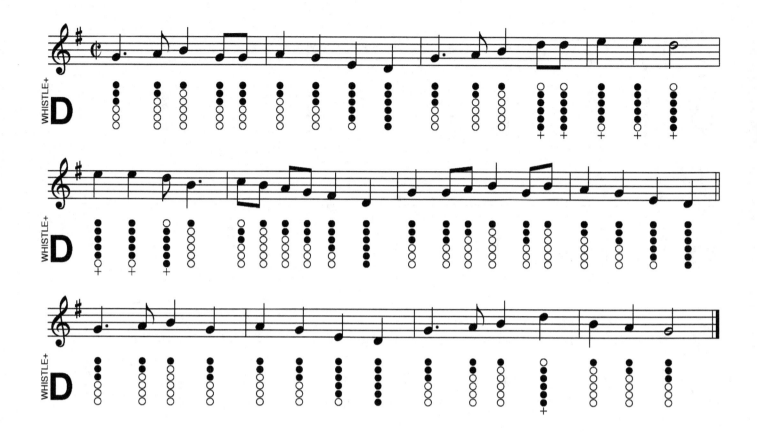

I'm a weaver, a Calton weaver,
I'm rash and a roving blade,
I've got silver in my pockets,
I'll go and follow the roving trade.

Oh. whisky, whisky, Nancy whisky,
Whisky, whisky, Nancy, oh!

As I cam' in by Glesca city,
Nancy Whisky I chanced to smell,
So I gaed in, sat doon beside her,
Seven lang years since I lo'ed her well.

The mair I kissed her, the mair I lo'ed her,
The mair I kissed her, the mair she smiled,
Soon I forgot my mither's teaching,
Nancy soon had me beguiled.

I woke up early in the morning,
To slake my drouth it was my need;
I tried to rise but I wasna able,
For Nancy had me by the heid.

Tell me landlady, whit's the lawin'?
Tell me whit there is to pay.
Fifteen shillings is the reckoning,
Pay me quickly and go away.

As I went oot by Glesca city
Nancy Whisky I chanced to smell:
I gaed in, drank four and sixpence
A twas left was a crooked scale.

I'll gang back to the Calton weaving
I'll surely mak' the shuttles fly
For I'll mak' mair at the Calton weaving
Than ever I did in a roving way.

Come all ye weavers, Calton weavers,
A' ye weavers, where e'er ye be;
Beware of whisky, Nancy whisky,
She'll ruin you as she ruincd me.

www.tradschool.com

Come O'er the Stream, Charlie

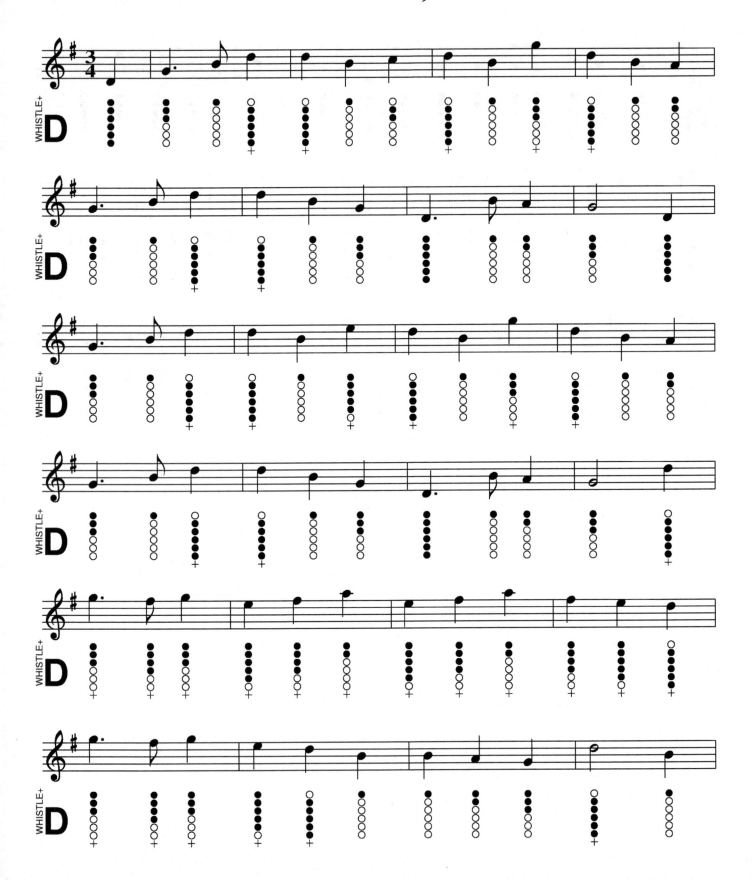

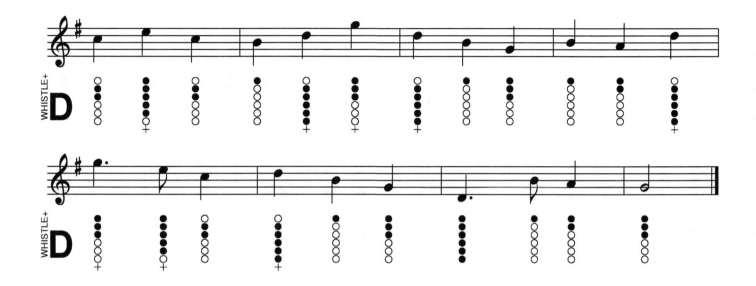

Come o'er the stream Charlie, dear Charlie, brave Charlie,
Come o'er the stream Charlie, and dine with MacLean;
And though you be weary, we'll make your heart cheery,
And welcome our Charlie and his loyal train.

We'll bring down the red deer, we'll bring down the black steer,
The lamb from the bracken and doe from the glen;
The salt sea we'll harry and bring to our Charlie,
The cream of the bothy, the curd from the pen.

And you shall drink freely the dews of Glensheerly,
That stream in the starlight: where kings dinna ken
And deep be your meed of the wine that is red,
To drink to your sire and his friend the MacLean.

It ought to invite you, or more will delight you,
'Tis ready a troop of our bold Highland men
Shall range on the heather, with bayonet and feather,
Strong arms and broad claymores, three hundred and ten.

Aiken Drum

There was a man lived in the moon, lived in the moon, lived in the moon,
There was a man lived in the moon,
And his name was Aiken Drum.

And he played upon a ladle, a ladle, a ladle,
And he played upon a ladle,
and his name was Aiken Drum.

And his hat was made of good cream cheese, of good cream cheese, of good cream cheese,
And his hat was made of good cream cheese,
And his name was Aiken Drum.

And his coat was made of good roast beef, of good roast beef, of good roast beef,
And his coat was made of good roast beef,
And his name was Aiken Drum.

And his buttons made of penny loaves, of penny loaves, of penny loaves,
And his buttons made of penny loaves,
And his name was Aiken Drum.

And his waistcoat was made of crust pies, of crust pies, of crust pies,
And his waistcoat was made of crust pies,
And his name was Aiken Drum.

And his breeches made of haggis bags, of haggis bags, of haggis bags,
And his breeches made of haggis bags,
And his name was Aiken Drum.

The Gypsy Laddies

Three gypsies cam tae oor hall door
And oh, but they sang bonny oh
They sang so sweet and too complete
That they stole the heart of our lady oh.

For she cam tripping down the stairs,
Her maidens too before her oh,
And when they saw her weel faured face
They throwed their spell oot owre her oh.

When her good lord came home that night
He was askin for his lady oh,
But the answer the servants gave tae him,
"She's awa wi the gypsy laddies oh".

Gae saddle tae me my bonnie, bonnie black,
My broon it's ne'er sae speedy oh.
That I may go ridin this long summer day
In search of my true lady oh"

But it's he rode east and he rode west
And he rode through Strathbogie oh
And there he met a gey auld man
That was comin through Strathbogie oh

For it's "Did ye come east or did ye come west
Or did you come through Strathbogie oh
And did ye see a gey lady?
She was followin three gypsy laddies oh"

For it's "I've come east and I've come west
And I've come through Strathbogie oh
And the bonniest lady that ere I saw
She was followin three gypsy laddies oh"

For the very last night that I crossed this river
I had dukes and lords to attend me oh.
But this night I must put in ma warm feet an wide,
An the gypsies widin before me oh.

Last night I lay in a good feather bed,
My own wedded lord beside me oh.
But this night I must lie in a cauld corn barn,
An the gypsies lyin aroon me oh.

For it's "Will you give up your houses and your lands,
An will you give up your baby oh?
An it's will you give up your own wedded lord
An keep followin the gypsy laddies oh?"

For it's "I'll give up my houses and my lands
An I'll give up my baby oh
An it's I will give up my own wedded lord
And keep followin the gypsy laddies oh"

For there are seven brothers of us all,
We all are wondrous bonnie oh
But this very night we all shall be hanged
For the stealin of the earl's lady oh.

Charlie is My Darling

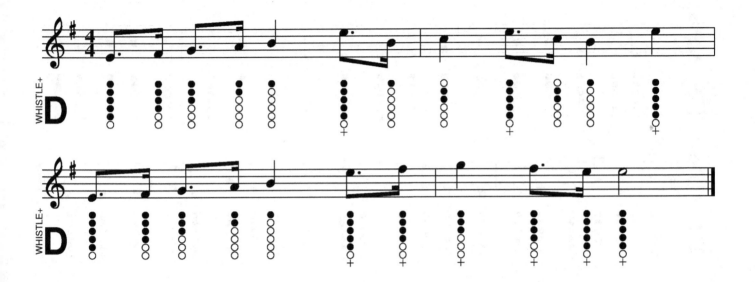

Charlie is my darling, my darling, my darling.
Charlie is my darling, the young Chevalier.

The Four Marys

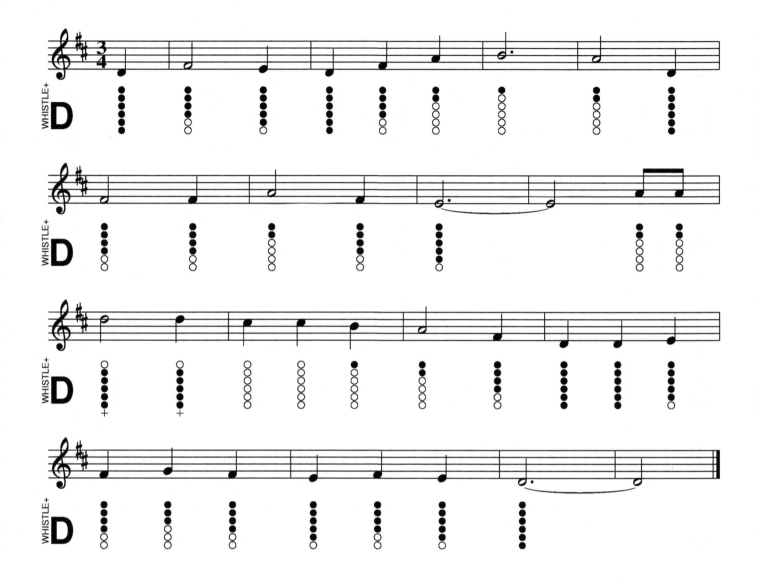

Last night there were four Marys
Tonight there'll be but three
There was Mary Seaton and Mary Beaton
And Mary Carmichael and me.

Oh, often have I dressed my Queen
And put on her braw silk gown
But all the thanks I've got tonight
Is to be hanged in Edinborough Town.

Full often have I dressed my Queen
Put gold upon her hair
But I have got for my reward
The gallows to be my share.

Oh, little did my mother know
The day she cradled me
The land I was to travel in
The death I was to dee.

Oh, happy, happy is the maid
That's born of beauty free
Oh, it was my rosy, dimpled cheeks
That's been the devil to me.

They'll tie a kerchief around my eyes
That I may not see to dee
And they'll never tell my father or mother
But that I'm across the sea.

The Blue Bells of Scotland

Oh where, tell me where is your Highland laddie gone?
Oh where, tell me where is your Highland laddie gone?
He's gone with streaming banners where noble deeds are done
And it's oh, in my heart I wish him safe at home

Oh where, tell me where did your Highland laddie dwell?
Oh where, tell me where did your Highland laddie dwell?
He dwelt in bonnie Scotland, where blooms the sweet blue bell
And it's oh, in my heart I love my laddie well

Oh what, tell me what does your Highland laddie wear?
Oh what, tell me what does your Highland laddie wear?
A bonnet with a lofty plume, and on his breast a plaid
And it's oh in my heart I love my Highland lad

Oh what, tell me what if your Highland lad be slain?
Oh what, tell me what if your Highland lad be slain?
Oh, no, true love will be his guard and bring him safe again
For it's oh, my heart would break if my Highland lad were slain

All the Blue Bonnets

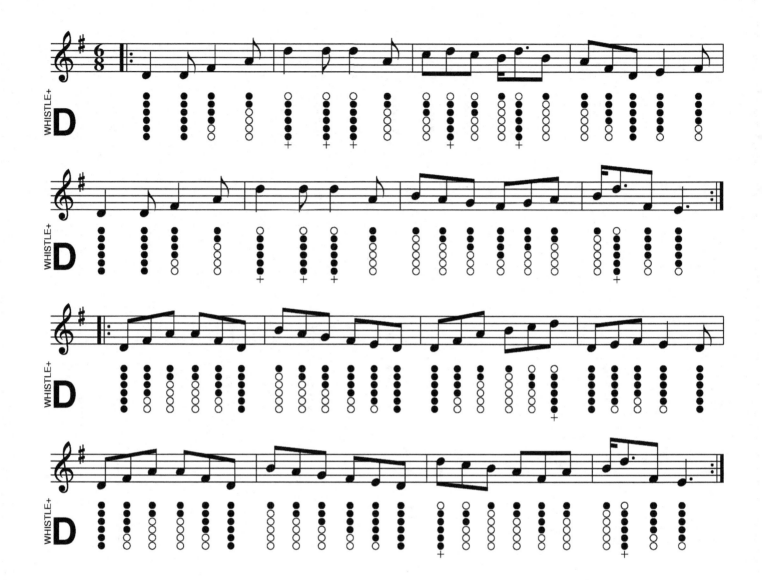

The Bonnie Banks of the Roses

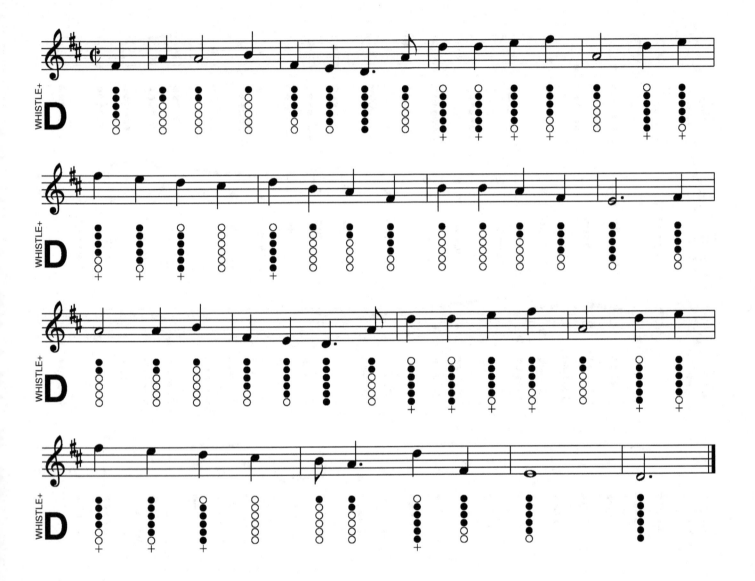

When I was a young thing, my mother used to say
That I'd be a roving lass and easy led astray;
Before I would work, sure, I'd rather sport and play
On the bonnie, bonnie banks of the roses.

On the banks of the roses, my love and I sat down,
He's taken out his German flute to play his love a tune;
In the middle of the tune, now, the bonnie lassie cried:
"O, it's Johnnie, dear, O Johnnie, don't leave me!"

For he's taken out a wee penknife as sharp as any lance,
And he's plunged it right to yon bonnie lassie's heart;
He plunged it right in to yon bonnie lassie's heart,
And he left her lying low among the roses.

Now, come all ye travelling lasses, a warning take by me,
It's never let a Gorgi lad an inch around your knee;
For if you do, you'll be sure to rue
For he'll leave you lying low among the roses.

The Skye Boat Song

Speed, bonnie boat, like a bird on the wing,
Onward! the sailors cry;
Carry the lad that's born to be King
Over the sea to Skye.

Loud the winds howl, loud the waves roar,
Thunderclouds rend the air;
Baffled, our foes stand by the shore,
Follow they will not dare.

Though the waves leap, so soft shall ye sleep,
Ocean's a royal bed.
Rocked in the deep, Flora will keep
Watch by your weary head.

Many's the lad fought on that day,
Well the Claymore could wield,
When the night came, silently lay
Dead on Culloden's field.

Burned are their homes, exile and death
Scatter the loyal men;
Yet ere the sword cool in the sheath
Charlie will come again.

www.tradschool.com

Wae's Me for Prince Charlie

A wee bird came tae our ha' door,
He warbled sweet and early,
And aye the outcome o' his lilt
Was "Wae's me for Prince Charlie."
Oh when I heard the bonnie, bonnie bird,
The tears came drappin' rarely.
I took my bonnet off my heid,
For weel I loved Prince Charlie.

On hills that are by right his ain,
He roams a lonely stranger.
On ilka hand he's pressed by want,
On ilka side by danger.
Yestere'en I met him in a glen,
My heart near bursted fairly,
For sadly changed indeed was he,
Oh, Wae's me for Prince Charlie.

Dark night came on, the tempest howled
Out o'er the hills and valleys,
And where was't that your Prince lay down,
Was him should be 'n a palace?
He rolled him in a hieland plaid,
Which covered him but sparely,
And slept beneath a bush o' broom,
Oh, Wae's me for Prince Charlie.

But now the bird saw some redcoats,
And he shook his wings wi' anger:
"o this is no land for me,
I'll tarry here nae laner."
A while he hover'd on the wing,
Ere he departed fairly:
But weel I mind the Fareweel strain;
'Twas "Wae's me for Prince Charlie!"

Dance to your Daddy

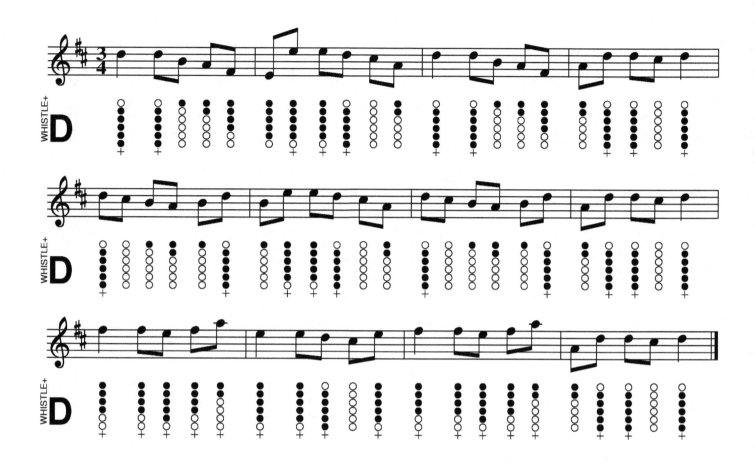

Dance to your daddy,
My bonnie laddie,
Dance to your daddy,
My bonnie lamb!

And you'll get a fishie
In a little dishie,
You will get a fishie,
When the boat comes home.

Dance to your daddy,
My bonnie laddie,
Dance to your daddy,
My bonnie lamb!

www.tradschool.com

McPherson's Rant

Fareweel, ye dungeons dark and strang,
Fareweel, fareweel tae ye,
MacPherson's time will no be lang
On yonder gallows tree

Sae rantinly and sae wantonly,
Sae dauntinly gaed he
For he played a tune and he danced aroon,
Below the gallows tree

It was by a woman's treacherous hand
That I was condemned tae dee
Above a ledge at a window she sat
And a blanket she threw ower me

There's some come here tae see me hang,
And some come tae buy my fiddle
But before that I would part wi her
I'd brak her through the middle

And he took the fiddle intae baith o' his hands
And he brak it ower a stane
Sayin, nay other hand shall play on thee
When I am dead and gane

The reprieve was comin ower the Brig o Banff
Te set MacPherson free,
But they pit the clock a quarter afore,
Ad they hanged him frae the tree.

The Barnyards of Delgaty

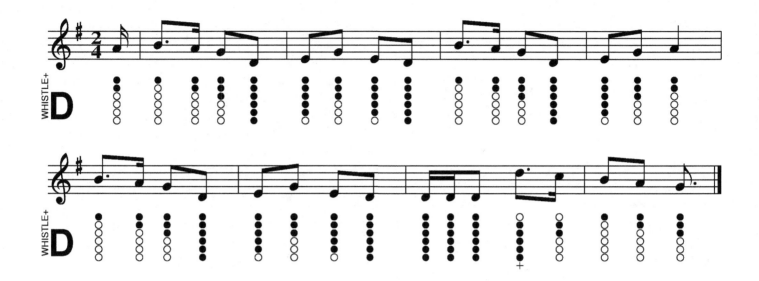

As ah gaed doon tae Turra Merket,
Turra Merket fur tae fee,
Ah met in wi a wealthy fairmer,
The Barnyards o Delgaty.

Linten adie, tooren adie,
Linten adie, tooren ay,
Linten lowerin lowerin lowerin,
The Barnyards o Delgaty.

He promised me the twa best horse
I ever set my een upon.
When ah gaed hame tae the Barnyards
There was nothin there but skin and bone.

The auld grey mare sat on her hunkers,
The auld dun horse lay in the grime.
For aa that I would 'hup' and cry,
They wouldna rise at yokin time.

When I gang tae the kirk on Sunday,
Mony's the bonny lass I see,
Sittin by her faither's side,
Winkin ower the pews at me.

Some can drink and no be drunk,
And some can fecht and no be slain.
I can coort anither man's lass,
And aye be welcome tae my ain.

Ma candle noo is fair brunt oot,
The snotter's fairly on the wane,
Fare ye weel, ye Barnyards,
Ye'll never catch me here again.

The Cradle Song

Scotland the Brave

The Bonnie Lass o'Fyvie

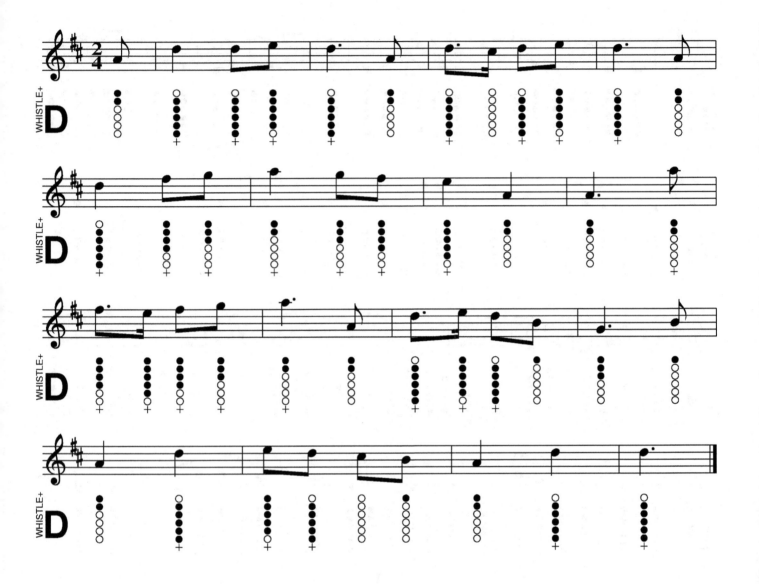

There once was a troop o' Irish dragoons
Cam marching doon through Fyvie-o
And the captain's fa'en in love wi' a very bonnie lass
And her name it was ca'd pretty Peggy-o

There's many a bonnie lass in the Howe o Auchterless
There's many a bonnie lass in the Garioch
There's many a bonnie Jean in the streets of Aiberdeen
But the floower o' them aw lies in Fyvie-o

O come doon the stairs, Pretty Peggy, my dear
Come doon the stairs, Pretty Peggy-o
Come doon the stairs, comb back your yellow hair
Bid a last farewell to your mammy-o

It's braw, aye it's braw, a captain's lady for to be
And it's braw to be a captain's lady-o
It's braw to ride around and to follow the camp
And to ride when your captain he is ready-o

O I'll give you ribbons, love, and I'll give you rings
I'll give you a necklace of amber-o
I'll give you a silken petticoat with flounces to the knee
If you'll convey me doon to your chamber-o

What would your mother think if she heard the guineas clink
And saw the haut-boys marching all before you o
O little would she think gin she heard the guineas clink
If I followed a soldier laddie-o

I never did intend a soldier's lady for to be
A soldier shall never enjoy me-o
I never did intend to gae tae a foreign land
And I never will marry a soldier-o

I'll drink nae more o your claret wine
I'll drink nae more o your glasses-o
Tomorrow is the day when we maun ride away
So farewell tae your Fyvie lasses-o

The colonel he cried, mount, boys, mount, boys, mount
The captain, he cried, tarry-o
O tarry yet a while, just another day or twa
Til I see if the bonnie lass will marry-o

Twas in the early morning, when we marched awa
And O but the captain he was sorry-o
The drums they did beat o'er the bonnie braes o' Gight
And the band played the bonnie lass of Fyvie-o

Long ere we came to Oldmeldrum toon
We had our captain to carry-o
And long ere we won into the streets of Aberdeen
We had our captain to bury-o

Green grow the birks on bonnie Ythanside
And low lie the lowlands of Fyvie-o
The captain's name was Ned and he died for a maid
He died for the bonnie lass of Fyvie-o

Will Ye No Come Back Again?

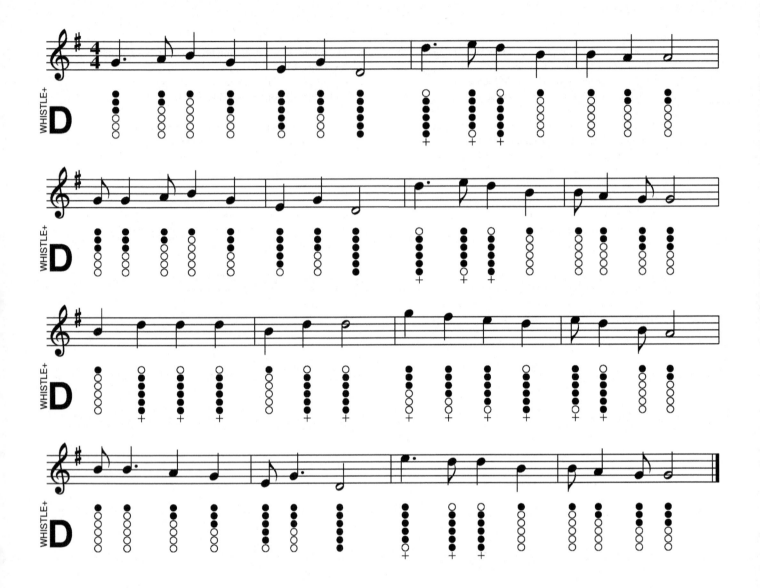

Bonnie Charlie's now awa'
Safely owre the friendly main;
Mony a heart will break in twa,
Should he ne'er come back again.

Will ye no come back again?
Will ye no come back again?
Better lo'ed ye canna be,
Will ye no come back again?

Ye trusted in your Hieland men,
They trusted you, dear Charlie.
They kent your hidin' in the glen,
Your cleadin was but barely.

English bribes were aa in vain,
An e'en tho puirer we may be;
Siller canna buy the heart
That beats aye for thine and thee.

Sweet's the laverock's note and lang,
Lilting wildly up the glen;
But aye to me he sings ae sang,
Will ye no come back again?

The Braes o'Killiecrankie

Whare hae ye been sae braw, lad!
Whare hae ye been sae brankie O?
Whare hae ye been sae braw, lad?
Cam ye by Killiecrankie O?

An ye had been whare I hae been,
Ye wad na been sae cantie O;
An ye had seen what I hae seen,
I'th' braes o' Killiecrankie O.

I faught at land, I faught at sea,
At hame I faught my Auntie, O;
But I met the Devil and Dundee
On th' braes o' Killiecrankie, O.

An ye had been whare I hae been,
Ye wad na been sae cantie O;
An ye had seen what I hae seen,
I'th' braes o' Killiecrankie O.

The bauld Pitcur fell in a furr,
An' Clavers gat a clankie, O;
Or I had fed an Athole Gled
On th' braes o' Killiecrankie, O.

An ye had been whare I hae been,
Ye wad na been sae cantie O;
An ye had seen what I hae seen,
I'th' braes o' Killiecrankie O.

www.tradschool.com

John Peel

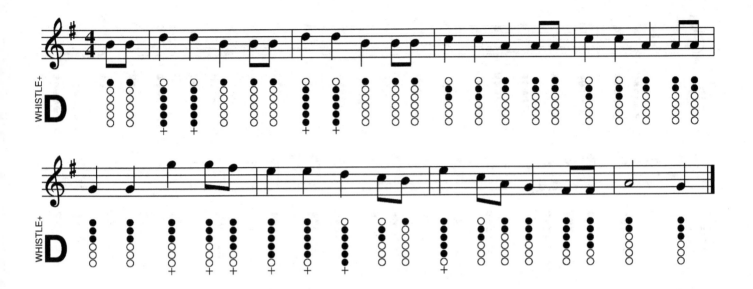

Do ye ken John Peel with his coat so gay?
Do ye ken John Peel at the break of day?
Do ye ken John Peel when he's far, far away
With his hounds and his horn in the morning.

Twas the sound of his horn brought me from my bed
And the cry of his hounds has me oftimes led
For Peel's view holloa would wake the dead
Or a fox from his lair in the morning.

Do ye ken that hound whose voice is death?
Do ye ken her sons of peerless faith
Do ye ken that a fox with his last breath
Cursed them all as he died in the morning?

Yes, I ken John Peel and auld Ruby, too
Ranter and Royal and Bellman so true
From the drag to the chase, from the chase to the view
From the view to the death in the morning.

APPENDIX : PLAYING THE TIN WHISTLE

You will find in the following pages some basic information to help you begin playing the tunes in this book on the whistle.

Holding the whistle

The whistle has 6 holes, which are covered with the first three fingers of each hand. The left hand fingers cover the top three holes, while the right hand covers the bottom (if you're left-handed, you may feel more comfortable with the right hand on top).

Grip the tip of the mouthpiece firmly between the lips (not the teeth) and rest the barrel on the thumbs; if held firmly at the mouthpiece, it shouldn't move. To make a sound, hold the whistle without covering any holes and blow a long, steady stream of air.

Tablatures & playing your first notes

In the tablatures that accompany the airs in this collection, the 6 holes of the whistle are represented by a diagram; open holes are indicated by white circles, while closed holes are black.

To play your first notes on the whistle, start with the C# (C sharp) which is played all holes open.

Then lower one finger at a time, starting with the left index (on the hole nearest the mouthpiece of the whistle) as in the diagram below:

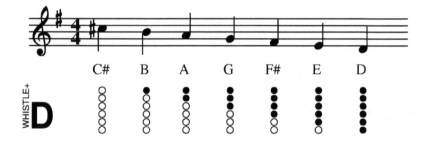

Be careful that the holes are properly covered, but without clenching the whistle too tightly - this will take some practise at the start. If a certain note doesn't play (or makes a creaking or squeaking sound) then it is probably because a hole is not properly covered and leaking air. If this happens, start at the top again and come back down.

The first octave

Here are all the notes of the first octave, starting with low D:

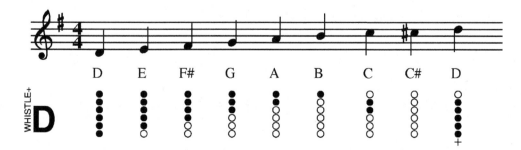

www.tradschool.com

123

The second octave

To play the second or higher octave, the fingering doesn't change except for the high D. For all other notes, you just need to blow slightly harder. On the fingering tablatures, the second octave is indicated by the plus symbol.

For the tunes in this collection, there is no need to play higher than the high B.

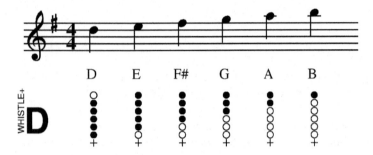

The scale of D :

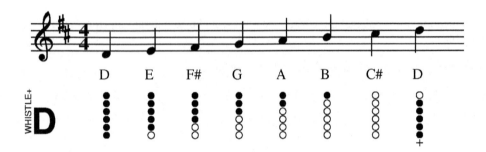

The scale of G

Here is the scale of G, with one new note, C natural.

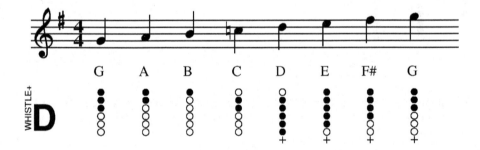

Here is the complete range of notes you will play on the tin whistle

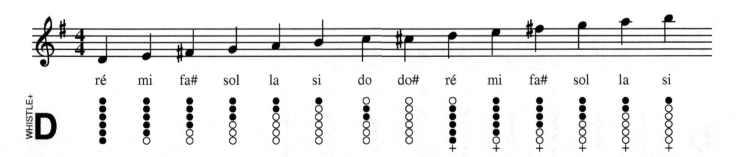

Index

A
- Aiken Drum 104
- All the Blue Bonnets 109
- An bhfaca tú mo Shéamaisín? 52
- Ar éirinn ní n-eósainn cé h-í 80
- Arthur McBride 8

B
- Báidín fheilimí 55
- Bantry Girl's Lament, The 33
- Bean Pháidín 56
- Beidh aonach amárach 82
- Bheir mé ó 87
- Black Velvet Band, The 44
- Blue Bells of Scotland, The 108
- Bonnie Banks of the Roses, The 110
- Bonnie Lass o'Fyvie, The 118
- Boolavogue 16
- Botany Bay 7
- Boys of Fairhill, The 11
- Braes o'Killiecrankie, The 121
- Buachaill ón Éirne 85
- Bunch of Thyme, A 42

C
- Cailin na gruaige doinne 78
- cailín rua, An 53
- Cailleach an airgid 73
- Calton Weaver, The 101
- Campbells are Coming, The 100
- Charlie is My Darling 106
- Cill Cháis 58
- Cliffs of Dooneen, The 22
- Come O'er the Stream, Charlie 102
- Coming Through the Rye 96
- Cradle Song, The 116
- Cuaichín Ghleann Néifin 57
- Cúnla 62

D
- Dance to your Daddy 113
- Danny Boy 30
- Déirín dé 72
- Do You Love an Apple 23
- Down by the Glenside 48
- Dúlamán na binne buí 86

E
- Eibhlín a rún 64

É
- Éamonn an chnoic 60

F
- Follow Me Up to Carlow 12
- Four Marys, The 107

G
- Galway Bay 34
- Galway Races, The 26
- Gin I Were 90
- Good Ship Kangaroo, The 6
- Green Grow the Rashes O 97
- Gypsy Laddies, The 105

H
- Harp that Once, The 10
- High Germany 25

I
- I'll Tell My Ma 32

J
- Jimmy mo mhíle stór 63
- John Peel 122
- Johnny I Hardly Know Ye 28

K
- Katie Bairdie 98

L
- Lanigan's Ball 36
- Lark in the Morning, The 40
- Last Rose of Summer, The 38
- Leaving of Liverpool, The 43
- Loch Lomond 99

M
- maidrín rua, An 74
- McPherson's Rant 114
- My Bonnie Lies Over the Ocean 94

N
- Nead na lachan sa mhúta 67
- Níl 'na lá 66

Ó
- Óró mo bháidín 76
- Óró! 'sé do bheatha 'bhaile 65

R
- Rare Old Mountain Dew, The 18
- Rising of the Moon, The 39

S
- Scotland the Brave 117
- Scots Wha Hae 92
- seanduine dóite, An 54
- Siúbhán Ní Dhuibhir 69
- Siúil a rún 68
- Skye Boat Song, The 111
- spailpín fánach, An 70

T
- Tá mé i mo shuí 84
- The Barnyards of Delgaty 115
- Thugamar féin an samhradh linn 71
- Trasna na dtonnta 75

W
- Wae's Me for Prince Charlie 112
- Waxie's Dargle, The 24
- Weile Waile 50
- Well Below the Valley, The 20
- Whiskey in the Jar 46
- Wild Mountain Thyme 91
- Wild Rover, The 14
- Will Ye No Come Back Again? 120

Y
- Ye Banks and Braes 93

ALSO AVAILABLE

Irish Music - 400 Traditional Tunes

184 pages, with audio download

Classic Irish Session Tunes from the author of "A Complete Guide to Playing Irish Traditional Music on the Whistle". A unique collection of the most popular tunes played in Ireland ... and throughout the world. Complete with 400-track audio download of each tune played at moderate speed on Tin Whistle.

Stephen Ducke is an Irish flute and whistle player from County Roscommon. Musician for over 30 years and an inspired teacher, he has recorded one solo album and is author and editor of several books of Irish and traditional music.

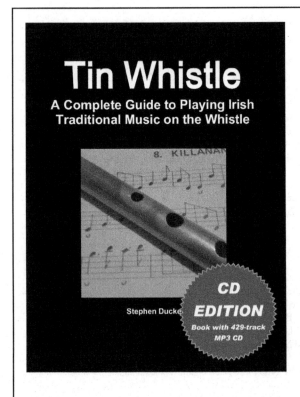

A Complete Guide to Playing Irish Traditional Music on the Whistle

286 pages; with 429 accompanying audio tracks

This tutor book, with its accompanying audio files, is intended to give a complete introduction to playing Irish music in the traditional style on the tin whistle; it covers all from the very first notes on the instruments to the most advances ornamentation. The book is broadly divided into two parts, with the shorter first part covering the basics of the whistle (pages 1-48) while the longer second part (pages 49-286) covers the playing of Irish traditional music on the instrument.

It is intended for anybody who wants to play traditional music in the Irish style, from complete beginners to confirmed or advanced players who wish to work on their style or ornamentation. Tablature as well as sheet music is used throughout the book, so it is accessible to the complete beginner; while more advanced players will appreciate the attention to detail in style and ornamentation in the later parts of the book.

www.tradschool.com

The Tunebook Series

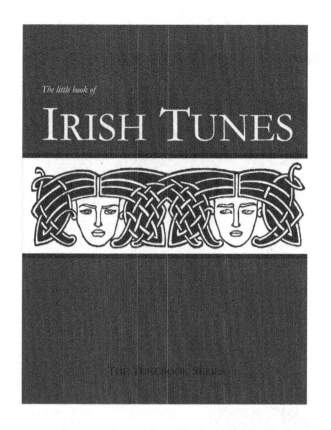
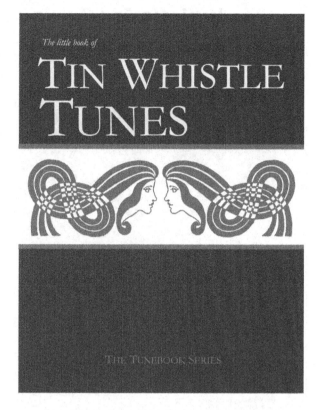

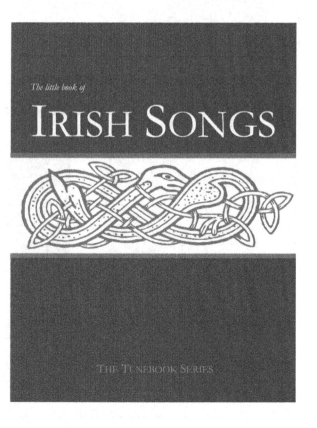

www.tradschool.com

TIN WHISTLE FOR BEGINNERS

Tin Whistle for Beginners : easy Irish songs and Tunes with fingering guides for Tin Whistle

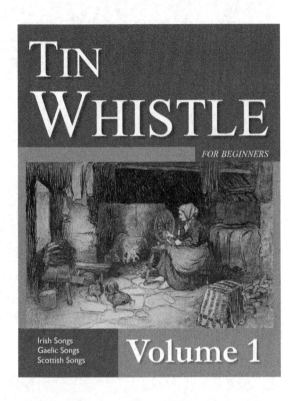
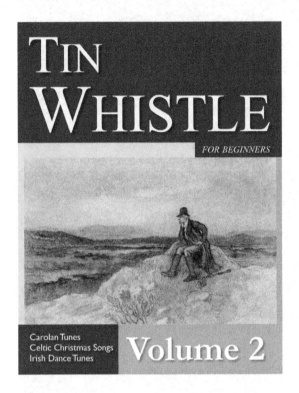

Whistle for Kids : easy tin whistle tunes for children

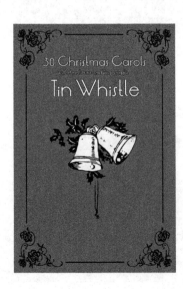
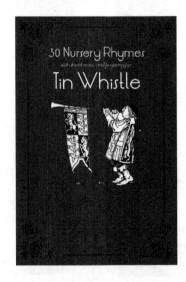

www.tradschool.com

CPSIA information can be obtained
at www.ICGtesting.com
Printed in the USA
LVOW04s1037110218
566109LV00028B/351/P